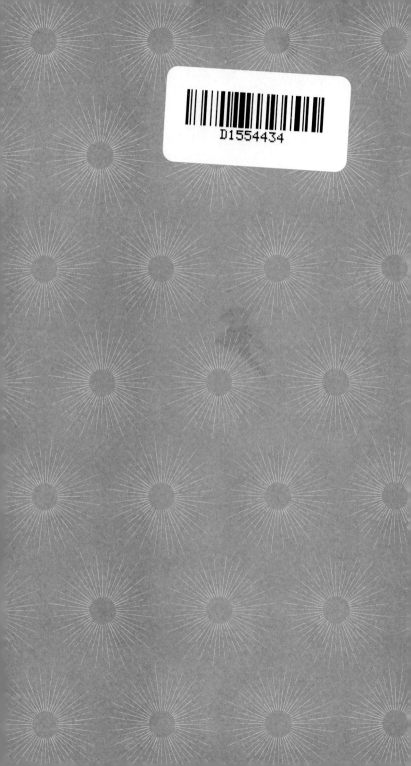

THE

HEAVENS

ARE

OPEN

THE
HEAVENS
ARE
OPEN

WENDY W. NELSON

DESERET BOOK

Salt Lake City, Utah

Library of Congress Cataloging-in-Publication Data

(CIP data on file)
ISBN 978-1-62972-715-8

Printed in the United States of America
Lake Book Manufacturing, Inc., Melrose Park, IL

10   9   8   7   6   5   4   3   2   1

For Russell

CONTENTS

CONTENTS

INTRODUCTION

SOME THINGS I BELIEVE

I am a believer.

I do not remember ever *not* believing in God, our Heavenly Father, and in His Son, Jesus Christ, and in the Holy Ghost.

I believe in

- the ministering of angels,
- dreams that bring messengers and messages,
- words from hymns that float into our minds unexpectedly and yet exactly when we need them, and
- scriptures that open to answer the questions we most need to have answered on a given day.

I believe in miracles. Actually, I count on them.

And, at this point in my life, I believe that the Lord brings us

- the precise miracles that will help us grow into our true selves, and
- miracles that will help us do His work.

I believe that in the temples of God we can receive His power through ordinances that

- enlighten our minds,
- invigorate our spirits,
- heal our hearts and bodies, and
- provide the eternal perspective that helps things make sense.

I believe in the power of priesthood blessings to heal. My widowed father was given a "death sentence" by a doctor—a specialist who told Dad that he had two weeks to live because the colon cancer (which had been excised seventeen months earlier) had metastasized to his liver, accompanied by total shutdown of his kidneys. My father was told to go home and to get his affairs in order.

Before he left the hospital, Dad received a priesthood blessing from my brother-in-law.

My father was at peace about his diagnosis and didn't want any "heroics," so he received no radiation, no chemotherapy, and no special diet (although we tried to get as many chocolate shakes into him as possible). He carried on serving others as he had done all of his kind, brilliant, gentle, and optimistic life, and he continued receiving hemodialysis for kidney failure. From time to time Dad would say, "Doctors can give you a diagnosis, but they should never give you a prognosis."

According to my father, his fifteen minutes of fame occurred on a September day *five months* after the doctor's two-week prognostication, when, because he was starting to look and feel better, I took him for an ultrasound-guided liver biopsy. My father's moment in the sun came when the doctor—who called in two other doctors because he couldn't believe what he was seeing on the ultrasound—said that he would not be able to do the biopsy. Why? Because there was no cancer present! The doctor then showed us the ultrasound pictures from April, clearly showing ten dark spots of cancer in the liver. And then he showed us the pictures from that September day. No spots. Dad lived *seven more years*, loving and learning every day, bringing joy to his family—and to his clients as he continued as their accountant—well into his eighty-second year of a wonderful life.

I also believe that there are times when the healing promised in a priesthood blessing is a complete and total healing—from the Lord's perspective. That blessing of healing translates into people being freed from *all* the suffering that accompanied their afflictions and from the vicissitudes of mortal life. How does that *complete healing* happen? They are taken Home. This was the case with my husband's daughter Wendy on January 11, 2019.

I believe in the power of prayer. As a grade-school child, I often wrote my prayers on the doors of my parents' wardrobe. It is fascinating to me that they never said a word to discourage me from this (although that was really so characteristic of my parents). That wardrobe was like a portal for me, linking me and my earthly worries—"Please help me get an A on my math test"—to heaven.

I believe in the power of fasting. When I was about nine years old, the principle of fasting resonated with me. So I began to fast for many of the tests I took. My parents never commented on what I was doing, just silently supported. I continued that practice through receiving my PhD degree. As I gained more experience with fasting, I learned that the Holy Ghost would bring all things to my memory as I increased my spiritual sensitivities to His whisperings. Fasting seemed like a good companion to my studying.

I believe in Jesus Christ's power to cleanse and

I BELIEVE

IN JESUS CHRIST'S POWER
TO CLEANSE AND HEAL, REDEEM
AND STRENGTHEN US. I AM SO
GRATEFUL TO OUR HEAVENLY
FATHER FOR HIS PLAN OF
HAPPINESS, OF CONTINUING
PROGRESSION, WHICH PROVIDED
A *Savior* FOR US.

heal, redeem and strengthen us. I am so grateful to our Heavenly Father for His plan of happiness, of continuing progression, which provided a Savior for us. And I will be forever indebted to Jesus Christ for coauthoring and editing my life history.

With all of that power available, and with my bedrock belief *in* all of that power, does that mean everything I have ever wanted in my life has happened? Hardly.

For example, I always knew that I would marry in my twenties and have ten children.

As it turns out, I married in my mid-fifties and am younger than the eldest of my husband's ten children.

The Lord was and is the Source of the love and hope and peace and joy that my husband and I feel now that we are together. Our covenants with God, including the new and everlasting covenant of marriage, become more real to us every day.

So, what helped when things didn't turn out as I originally hoped or planned? First and foremost, I knew my parents loved me. That certainty cut through everything. Then, regularly doing all the spiritually strengthening things that you and I know to do kept me moving ahead: praying, fasting, serving others, fulfilling Church assignments, and spending time in the temple and in the scriptures.

Often the Lord's counsel to the Prophet Joseph Smith helped me to look beyond the present during disappointing, really tough, even frightening times: "All these things shall give thee experience, and shall be for thy good" (Doctrine and Covenants 122:7).

And how has my life been blessed by various un-expected experiences? What are some of the things I learned?

I learned about the reality of life after death when my long-awaited baby brother, David, lived only seven hours. On that first day of my fifth-grade year, September 1, I was thrilled with the Polaroid picture my dad had taken of David that morning when he was born and immediately placed in an oxy-gen tent. I took that photo with me to school to show all my friends. Later that day, as I walked home, I knocked on every door I passed and asked, "Would you like to see a picture of my baby brother?" I was elated, and our neighbors in Raymond, Alberta, Canada, were so welcoming.

When I arrived home, I learned that David had died. I was grief stricken. That's when my grand-mother took me into a private room where she and I could be together to talk and to cry. She told me that she had been inconsolable when her grand-mother Sarah had died. Then, several months later, Sarah—now living on the other side of the veil—visited Grandma. Sarah sat right on Grandma's bed. She told my grandmother to stop grieving and get on with her life. Sarah was very much alive and well.

From that moment on, even though I was sad—and became even sadder when I saw how sad my mother was—I knew that David was alive. He was my brother and would always be my brother. David had come to earth and received a body, and now he was helping the Lord build up the kingdom of God on the other side of the veil.

I learned that irony truly is "the hard crust on the bread of adversity," as Elder Neal A. Maxwell taught.[1] I learned this when my mother—the woman who had taught others to open their eyes to see so many of the beauties around them—became blind!

This seemed tragically ironic, as it was my mother who would phone me from 150 miles away and say, "Run out and look at the moon!" It was my mother who would call a neighbor and say, "Let's drive out to the Sugar Factory Lake and watch the Canada geese return."

Mom was fascinated with nature and the solar system. A big fat yellow moon rising up from the prairie horizon stirred her soul, as did the thinnest crescent moon high in the sky. From the aurora borealis to a robin in the rain, no constellation or creature seemed to go unnoticed by my mother's all-seeing eyes.

And now she couldn't see! My dad helped her with her makeup and curled her hair. Friends wrote letters for her that she wished she could write, and, in order to continue to learn, she listened to books on tape. For such an independent woman, accepting help from others involved a steep learning curve for Mom. But she learned, and those who helped her were also blessed because she found every opportunity to teach and lift them. And she was so much fun!

I had the privilege of being at her bedside on the spring morning when she departed. I pictured her bolting through the veil of death *so* eager to *see* her son David and other family members and friends on the other side.

I learned about the rewards of strict obedience and the power of patriarchal blessings when my older sister, Kathy, at the age she thought she would be getting married, ended her relationship with her boyfriend. He was a seemingly wonderful man whom she had thought she was going to marry, but he was not a member of The Church of Jesus Christ of

Latter-day Saints. And, despite my sister's example, teachings, and prayers, and those of our parents, he was making no movement toward joining. Kathy bravely took counsel from words in her patriarchal blessing that told her to marry *only* in the temple.

Saying good-bye to her nonmember boyfriend was a colossal leap of faith for Kathy, as all of her friends (girls and boys) were now married. It seemed that all the great Latter-day Saint men had "been taken."

But the Lord provided. Kathy married a good man. They had a lot in common in terms of what they valued: faith, family, service, education, and hard work. And their love grew as they served the Lord and their family. He became the stake patriarch even before he was called as stake president. Kathy served as president of various auxiliaries at the ward and stake level and as a temple ordinance worker. Together they raised five terrific children and now have seventeen fabulous grandchildren. At one point they served as temple president and matron, and later they served a temple mission together in another country. I believe Kathy's stake patriarch saw just how important the temple would be in her life, and that informed his prophetic counsel for her to marry *only* in the temple.

I have learned and continue to learn about

courage, determination, indefatigability, and resiliency by observing how my younger sister lives her life. She has battled for the very breath of life literally all of her life.

Virginia was born with a rare congenital anomaly that resulted in a chronic lung condition. Undaunted, she studied and received two master's degrees, worked full-time for nearly twenty-five years at Brigham Young University, and served as organist as well as Primary pianist in whatever stake and ward in which she has lived. She is one of my heroes. The powers of heaven have sustained her—helping her day after day to do the impossible, to never complain, and to find joy and beauty in each day.

I have learned how the Lord orchestrates our lives when we are seeking to do His will. When we want to fill the measure of our creation more than we want things of the world, the heavens will open.

Michael McLean's lyrics are true for me:

All I ever wanted, all I ever dreamed of,
Everything I hoped, and all the things I prayed for
Couldn't hold a candle to what I've been given,
I've been given what I need.[2]

Although all I've been given hasn't necessarily been all that I *thought* I wanted, the Lord has known exactly *what* I have needed as well as *when* I needed

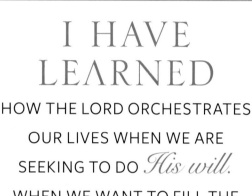

I HAVE
LEARNED

HOW THE LORD ORCHESTRATES

OUR LIVES WHEN WE ARE

SEEKING TO DO *His will.*

WHEN WE WANT TO FILL THE

MEASURE OF OUR CREATION

MORE THAN WE WANT

THINGS OF THE WORLD,

the heavens will open.

those blessings. What I have *always* needed, what I have sought for, has been for the heavens to open for me.

Here are just a few of the things I've discovered:

The heavens open when we seek. I am inspired to seek more diligently and with more enthusiasm every time I recall the following words of the Prophet Joseph Smith, the Lord's prophet of this last dispensation:

"The things of God are of deep import; and time, and experience, and careful and ponderous and solemn thoughts can only find them out. Thy mind, O man! if thou wilt lead a soul unto salvation, must stretch as high as the utmost heavens, and search into and contemplate the darkest abyss, and the broad expanse of eternity—thou must commune with God."[3] The heavens don't always open quickly, but they *will* ultimately open.

I've learned that *the heavens will open*
- *when we take a question to general conference,*
- *when we take a question to the scriptures,*[4]
- *when we pray with real intent and faith in Christ,* and
- *when we make a sacrifice to the Lord.*

For example, when I followed the counsel of President Russell M. Nelson to participate for ten days in a "fast from social media and from any other media that bring negative or impure thoughts to your mind,"[5] I could tell *such* a difference after only ten days that I decided to extend the experience. So, a couple of months later, I commenced an eleven-week fast from TV and movies (except for watching a rare show of some kind with my husband) in preparation for the next general conference. I couldn't believe how the heavens opened for me when I didn't have the competing ideas and noise of the world in my mind.

The heavens will open when we open our computers to do family history research—so much so that I have learned to keep a pad of paper close by to capture thoughts that come to me as I seek the qualifying information for my ancestors.

The heavens are more likely to open when we have faith that they will. When we truly believe they *will* open, miracles happen.

President Nelson taught: "In the absence of experiences with God, one can doubt the existence of God. So, put yourself in a position to begin having experiences with Him."[6]

We could paraphrase his words and say that in the absence of having experiences with the heavens opening for us, we could doubt that the heavens *will ever* open for us, and we could doubt that they actually open for others.

However, it is my testimony that the heavens *are* open.

They are open for the prophet of the Lord, and they are open for each and every one of us as we do the requisite spiritual work.

CHAPTER 1

REMOVE CONTENTION

I learned early in our marriage that my husband was exquisitely sensitive to contention. If we were watching a movie and the characters began to argue or fight, he would turn the movie off. If a basketball or football game morphed from healthy competition to a contest filled with angry slurs and fighting—on the field or in the stands—again, he was not pleased.

Contention blocks revelation. Contention prevents the heavens from opening for us. Remember the Prophet Joseph Smith's account of a day when there was contention between him and Emma? What was the effect? Joseph was not able to translate until the contention was put away. Let's talk about how to remove contention from our lives so the heavens can open for us.

Driving along Interstate 15 in Utah, you can see billboards and lighted signs announcing Utah's safe-driving campaign slogan: "zero fatalities." This goal of zero fatalities is all about eliminating deaths on our roadways.

As the campaign indicates: "Some say it's impossible. But if we all work together, we can reach zero fatalities."

Each time I see the slogan "zero fatalities," I drive a bit more carefully.

The "zero fatalities" slogan reminds me of the Savior's message to the Nephites in which He taught His doctrine of "zero contention":

"He that hath the spirit of contention is not of me, but is of the devil, who is the father of contention, and he stirreth up the hearts of men to contend with anger, one with another. Behold, this is not my doctrine, . . . but this is my doctrine, that such things should be done away" (3 Nephi 11:29–30).

Jesus Christ makes it clear that He does not like anger. We cannot come close to Him, or even think of coming close to Him, our Savior and Redeemer, when we are experiencing *any* contention with *anyone!*

He wants us first to be reconciled with *everyone*, including our spouses, our parents and siblings, our in-laws, our coworkers, and our children (see 3 Nephi 12:22–24). And then we can come closer to Him than we ever have in our lives.

Just as the safe-driving slogan of "zero fatalities" invites us to drive more safely, the Savior's doctrine of "zero contention" invites us to begin putting contention away—removing it from our hearts, our minds, our conversations, and our homes. It invites us to be intentional about looking for ways to resolve problems without allowing our differences of opinion to disintegrate into acrimony or anger.

When we are really trying to be safer drivers, when we drive in a manner to support the zero-fatalities goal, we realize there are things we can do differently when we drive. And we start doing them.

In like manner, when we are earnestly seeking zero contention, the Spirit will show us how to avoid contention, how to be reconciled with others—even if, at present, that goal seems absolutely impossible!

You may, at this point, be rolling your eyes and thinking: *You just don't understand the contentious person I have to deal with!* But think of this: The Savior did not say, "Please put contention away— *unless* the person with whom you are contending is a really difficult, mean, ornery, prideful, obnoxious person."

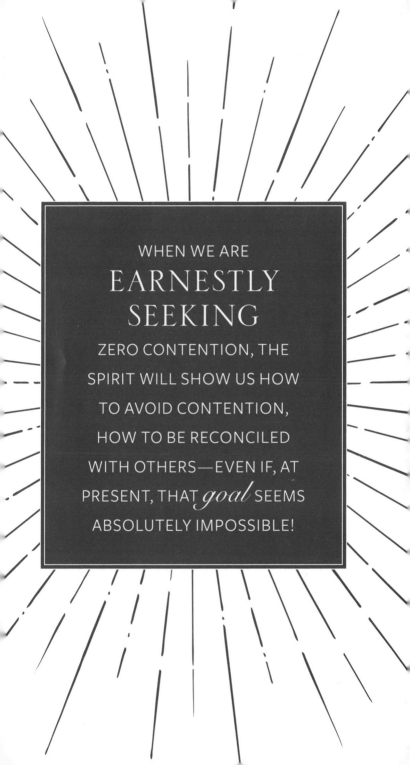

WHEN WE ARE
EARNESTLY
SEEKING
ZERO CONTENTION, THE
SPIRIT WILL SHOW US HOW
TO AVOID CONTENTION,
HOW TO BE RECONCILED
WITH OTHERS—EVEN IF, AT
PRESENT, THAT *goal* SEEMS
ABSOLUTELY IMPOSSIBLE!

No, the Savior taught that contention is to be done away. Period.

And the great, reassuring news is that we know the Lord never asks us to do anything without making it possible for us to do it (see 1 Nephi 3:7). That means the Savior Himself will provide a way for us to put contention away.

Chapters 11 through 17 of 3 Nephi are filled with the Savior's teachings about how to remove contention from our hearts and minds—how to build great relationships. Decades ago, as a marriage and family therapist, I prayerfully studied the Savior's words in those chapters and found woven throughout them many truths that I knew would help people build strong relationships and even heal ravaged ones. Truths such as:

- the importance of using a softer voice;
- the importance of repeating loving words—even when others don't respond;
- the power that our thoughts have on others to influence them—positively or negatively;
- the importance of commending others in public;
- the importance of handling with extreme care and love the first few minutes when we are with someone—for example, the first few minutes in the morning and the first few

minutes when we come back together at the end of the day.

As we prayerfully study the scriptures, praying for the Holy Ghost to be with us, we can bring to the Lord all our questions about how to avoid contention and heal our relationships. We will be led along.

For example, the Spirit might teach us how to avoid or prevent a confrontation by anticipating an interaction in advance. We might learn how to respond with love rather than anger, even when provoked. We can pray *right in the moment* to be given an extra measure of patience or compassion for a person who is lashing out in anger.

The scriptures are filled with inspiring examples of those who were serious about living the Savior's doctrine of zero contention. One of my favorites is the story of Moroni and Pahoran.

In the latter part of the book of Alma, we read the account of Captain Moroni, the leader of the Nephite armies, and Pahoran, the governor of the land. Moroni and Pahoran are on the same team. Tensions are building. Moroni's armies need supplies and reinforcements; in fact, they are in serious trouble. And the help they are expecting to receive from the government never arrives.

Moroni writes a scathing letter to Pahoran,

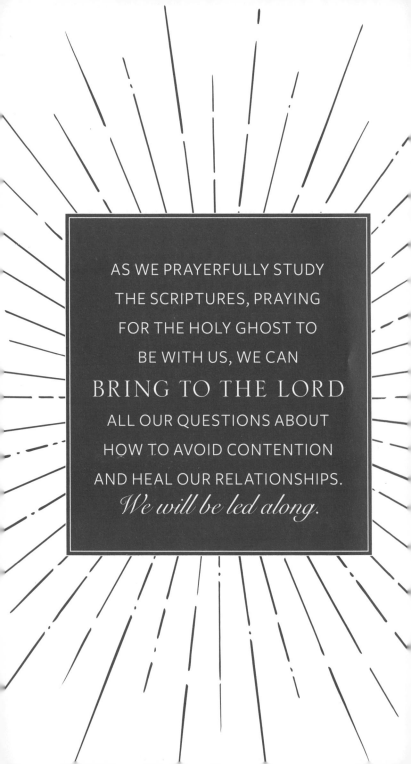

AS WE PRAYERFULLY STUDY
THE SCRIPTURES, PRAYING
FOR THE HOLY GHOST TO
BE WITH US, WE CAN
BRING TO THE LORD
ALL OUR QUESTIONS ABOUT
HOW TO AVOID CONTENTION
AND HEAL OUR RELATIONSHIPS.
We will be led along.

accusing him of neglecting the armies. His message includes such inflammatory phrases as: "Great has been your neglect towards us," and "Can you think to sit upon your thrones in a state of thoughtless stupor, while your enemies are spreading the work of death around you?" and "It is because of your iniquity that we have suffered so much loss" (Alma 60:5, 7, 28).

Moroni goes on and on in his epistle outlining all Pahoran's presumed neglect. His tone and accusations are ruthless and relentless.

Pahoran's response is one for the ages. In his reply, he explains his circumstances to Moroni: "I say unto you, Moroni, that I do not joy in your great afflictions, yea, it grieves my soul. But behold, there are those who *do* joy in your afflictions, yea, insomuch that they have risen up in rebellion against *me*" (Alma 61:2–3; emphasis added).

Then comes one of my favorite responses of all time. Pahoran lives the Savior's doctrine of zero contention when he says: "Now, in your epistle you have censured me, but it mattereth not; I am not angry" (Alma 61:9).

If Pahoran had stopped there, his response would have been fabulous! He fully acknowledged the reprimands and accusations of Moroni, and then he said that all of those criticisms and accusations didn't matter—and that he wasn't even angry.

The natural man would be angry and would likely respond to the false accusations with the same amount of venom, maybe even more. That natural-man response could perpetuate an escalating and never-ending cycle of contention.

But Pahoran has put off the natural man. He demonstrates that he is a true follower of Jesus Christ when he says, "it mattereth not; I am not angry."

And he doesn't leave it at that. Pahoran goes on to say something truly inspiring—something that is absolutely *not* of this world. His next words stop the contention and heal the situation instantly.

What does he say?

To his reassurance, "it mattereth not; I am not angry," he adds, "but [I] do rejoice in the greatness of your heart" (Alma 61:9). Imagine: *"But [I] do rejoice in the greatness of your heart!"* Wow!

Those words draw my heart to Pahoran's. Because those words came from the depths of Pahoran's own great heart, surely Moroni's heart was softened.

What was the outcome? Contention was put away!

What a pattern Pahoran gives us! Perhaps he even gives us the very words we can use when we are attacked, criticized, or falsely accused. If we are sincere about learning how to live the Savior's doctrine of zero contention, perhaps we can find a time to practice saying something like:

"Now, in your email or text, you have censured (criticized/attacked/reprimanded/falsely accused) me, but it doesn't matter; I am not angry, but do rejoice in the greatness of your heart."

Or across the dinner table:

"Now, as we've been talking, you have censured (criticized/attacked/reprimanded/falsely accused) me, but it doesn't matter; I am not angry, but do rejoice in the greatness of your heart."

We can pray—*even in the moment*—to have eyes to see our attacker, our accuser, our contender as the Savior sees him or her. We can pray to see—if we pray and persist long enough—the goodness, even the greatness, of the other person's heart.

Now, back to the safe-driving slogan of "zero fatalities." That's the goal—zero fatalities—and yet people still get killed on Utah roads.

However, the goal remains the same. They haven't changed the slogan to: "Let's try for only 100 fatalities this year!" No, zero fatalities is the goal.

The doctrine of the Savior is "zero contention"

—*zero*—and yet, misunderstandings happen. Feelings get hurt. Contentions arise.

What do we do then?

We can continue to keep the Savior's doctrine of zero contention at the forefront of our minds and in our hearts. We can pray to see *our* part—is there anything we are unintentionally doing that is fueling the contention? When all is said and done, we can control only our own behavior and reactions. Thus, *we* can be the ones to repent. *We* can apologize. *We* can resist the urge to judge. *We* can pray to understand the other person's point of view.

And *we* can forgive.

We can pray to do everything that is possible to put the contention away.

We can pray again to see the great heart of the other person, and perhaps we can use a softer voice.

Our goal is to learn to speak about *anything and everything* in a manner that allows the Spirit to be present. If we do, contention *will* be put away.

As we follow each and every impression that comes to us as we pray to live the Savior's doctrine of zero contention, peace will come.

For example, one young mother was guided to have recordings of the Book of Mormon playing in the background when their children came home from school at what had previously been termed in their home the "arsenic hour." The words of the Book of Mormon wafting through the air brought a new calm, even a new feeling of peace to their home. This young mother was astonished at the power of words of the Book of Mormon to put contention away.

A husband and wife who both worked outside the home quickly realized that at the end of the day when they returned home from work, they needed a few minutes to decompress from the pressures they had been under that day. They often accomplished this by kneeling together and praying before they did anything else.

You and I are children of loving Heavenly Parents who long to have us back Home clean, qualified, and free of contention. As we keep our covenants with increasing exactness, we have access to the power of Jesus Christ made available to us because of His Atonement. That power will heal our hearts and hurts, help us repent, and magnify our abilities to live the Savior's doctrine of zero contention. Zero contention is a crucial ingredient for opening the heavens.

CHAPTER 2

FOCUS ON WHAT MATTERS

I belong to The Church of Jesus Christ of Latter-day Saints.

There is an urgency embedded even in the name of the Lord's Church. Because we are living in the latter days before the Savior's return, *how* we spend our time here on earth really matters.

President Henry B. Eyring, Second Counselor in the First Presidency of the Church, learned that truth at the young age of thirteen. His family had just moved from Princeton, New Jersey, to Utah. He didn't really like school in Utah—people made fun of his accent, and he had no close friends. He wasn't even finding joy in basketball, for which he had a natural talent.

At that point, life was tough for young Henry.

In a moment of self-pity, an impression came to his mind. A spiritual voice spoke a warning. As he described it: "I felt, not heard, a voice. It was an impression, which I knew then was from God. It was this thought, and close to these words: 'Someday, when you know who you really are, you will be sorry you didn't use your time better.'"

He continued: "I thought then that the impression was odd, since I thought I was using my time pretty well, and I thought I knew who I was. Now, years later, I am beginning to know who I am, and who you are, and why we will be so sorry if we do not invest our time well."[7]

We are stewards of our time. We need to invest our time well.

What does that mean?

Do you remember a TV advertisement for a certain vegetable drink? The company had many versions of it. Each iteration invited us to wake up to what we were eating or drinking as snacks.

In one version, a mother excitedly talks to her baby daughter about the French fry the mother is eating. The baby girl looks concerned, even incredulous, as the mother continues to speak about how fabulous the French fry is. Then the ad shows the baby giving the mother a little whack on the forehead to bring her mother to her senses, reminding her what she could have had instead.

That baby was inviting her mother to wake up to what she was putting into her body!

Have you ever had a wake-up call that helped you see that you could have made a better life choice?

Perhaps the number on the scale in the morning after a late-night snacking binge served as a wake-up call. *"Why did I think that eating pancakes at midnight was such a great idea? What was I thinking?"* (I can't imagine why I would so quickly come up with that example!)

Perhaps you've had a wake-up call that let you know you've been missing out on something. A friend called one day having had a major wake-up call of that nature. "I've been studying the scriptures and statements from our leaders about women in the Church, and in particular, the access we have as women to the divine power of the priesthood," she said. "As I've studied, I have thought, 'Where have I been all my life? Why have I never known that we as women are actually endowed with power in the house of the Lord or that through ordinances we have direct access to priesthood power?'"

My friend is, and always has been, a faithful Latter-day Saint woman. She is a dedicated wife, mother, and grandmother. She has served in leadership callings in the Church and taught Gospel Doctrine; she studies her scriptures daily; she loves the temple and attends at least weekly. But truths that were brought to her heart and mind by the Holy Ghost let her know that she had only been skimming the surface of what was possible in her life.

Our conversation that day brought to my mind Brigham Young's declaration that "we live far beneath our privileges." His fuller wisdom stated: "If a person lives according to the revelations given to God's people, he may have the Spirit of the Lord to signify to him his will, and to guide and to direct him in the discharge of his duties, in his temporal as well as his spiritual exercises. I am satisfied, however, that in this respect *we live far beneath our privileges*."[8]

Perhaps you've had a wake-up call that let you know how time and your life are passing by. I visited an elderly friend of mine and realized that I am now the same age she was when I first met her two decades ago. I was shocked! *What? That couldn't be true! Wasn't that just a few years ago? How did that happen? Where did those years go?*

I was also jarred awake by noticing that she had some of the same unmet goals I have. She still had the same clothes hanging in her closet that she was going to have altered almost twenty years ago. And so do I!

Perhaps laboratory results at a visit to our doctor wake us up to how quickly our health is deteriorating and how urgent it is that we make lifestyle changes. Perhaps an accident or a brush with death wakes us up to the truth that our zooming-around life is spiraling out of control.

Perhaps a long-overdue, but finally true and humble, accounting of our finances wakes us up to the financial straits we are in because we have not been living the Lord's law of finance to pay the Lord 10 percent first, and we have not heeded the counsel of our leaders to put money away for the future.

Perhaps we are called upon, without any prior notice, to provide spiritual comfort and strength to someone we love, and we wish in that moment that we were better prepared spiritually. We wish we had been more regular in our personal prayers, scripture study, and time in the temple.

Sometimes a pivotal event in the Church can wake us up. I think of two great biological sisters who were young single adults at the time I met them. They lived in Moscow, Russia. I talked with them prior to a meeting for women the day before

President Russell M. Nelson (then Elder Nelson) was to create the first stake in Russia in Moscow.

I asked them, "What does it mean to you that you are going to have a stake in Russia?"

They answered quickly and in unison: *"This is serious!"*

And the proof of how seriously they were taking the restored gospel of Jesus Christ and His Church, from that moment on, is that two years later they were both serving missions as full-time representatives of the Lord.

I appreciate one of the positive messages in a movie from more than twenty years ago. *Groundhog Day* (1993) is an American fantasy comedy film in which an arrogant, egocentric TV weatherman finds himself in a time loop when covering the annual Groundhog Day event in Punxsutawney, Pennsylvania. As a result, he lives the same day over and over again. After indulging in everything from hedonism to thoughts of suicide, he begins to reexamine his life and priorities.

Things begin to change, but *only when* he starts to *serve* people instead of *using* them. He catches a boy falling from a tree, helps some women with a flat tire, saves a man from choking to death, helps a young couple recommit to marriage. He develops skills he'd never even considered before. He learns to make ice sculptures—beautifully; learns to play the piano—superbly; enhances his speaking abilities—noticeably. His capacity and happiness grow as he uses his time well.

Perhaps, like that hapless weatherman, when we find ourselves thinking, "Oh, here we go again," or, "Didn't we just do this?" or, "Same old, same old," all embedded within a sigh of resignation, we need to wake up. Shake things up.

Wake-up calls can be so motivating, moving us to take the next steps to really turn a corner in our lives, to truly repent. Have you had a wake-up call recently that let you know it is time to

> Change
> Adapt
> Adjust
> Amend
> Repent
> Recalibrate
> Revamp
> Reform
> Revise
> Reboot your life?

I have!

I had a wake-up call about the use of my time. I was not prepared for it—in fact, I was totally caught

WAKE-UP CALLS
CAN BE SO MOTIVATING,
MOVING US TO TAKE
THE NEXT STEPS TO REALLY
turn a corner IN OUR
LIVES, TO TRULY REPENT.

off guard by it! The wake-up call was confusing to me, and it took a bit of time to sort it out.

It was the summer of 2010. One of my dearest lifelong friends, Barbara, died, and I spoke at her funeral in Canada. When I returned home to Utah, I was ready to tackle a big project: the dejunking of my side of our garage. The task had seemed *so* overwhelming to me that had I left it—for four years!

However, I was now armed with the question, "Would Barbara care about this file (or this article, or these presentation materials) now that she lives on the other side of the veil?" With that added measure of perspective, I was finally ready to sort through thirty years of my former professional life.

All through the day and into the night for about ten days (Sunday excluded), I sorted, tossed out, and shredded. And I did some condensed and intense reminiscing as well. Through that rigorous process, I whittled more than a hundred boxes down to thirty! You may know what that's like. It was rigorous!

My husband was so supportive: encouraging me, bringing me fresh garbage bags to fill, bringing me food and water, and making new labels for the boxes that survived the purging. His smiles got bigger with each additional box I cleared out.

And then finally, on the last Saturday of that

July, one of our friends arrived with his long-bed pickup at the prescheduled time of 7:00 p.m.—quite literally as I tossed the very last file into the garbage.

Aaahhh. Success! Let the bells ring out and the banners fly! I was almost expecting confetti and balloons to fall from the ceiling of the garage as part of the celebration to punctuate the completion of this arduous, long-overdue task.

Instead, along with lots of joy and even more relief, there was a little something nudging its way into my rejoicing. A little pit in my stomach was starting to grow. What *was* that?

In the midst of all the intense, emotion-packed experiences of that July, one thing had gone missing from my life: my regular time in the temple. I could feel that I needed to be there. I *wanted* to be there. And yet, I was so exhausted at the end of each day, I didn't feel like getting all cleaned up to go to the temple.

Also I reasoned (read: *rationalized*) that the Bountiful Utah Temple was closed for two weeks for regular maintenance cleaning—and it would, after all, take me all of *seventeen minutes* to drive to the Salt Lake Temple from my home. (I successfully pushed to the back of my mind the true accounts of Latter-day Saints who travel several days on boats and buses—one way—in order to get to the temples in their countries.)

Thus, it had been several weeks since I had been in the temple. It felt as though I was losing power—enabling power, protecting power, healing power, all the kinds of power that we need as we move through the "spook-alley experiences" of this life (as Truman G. Madsen so aptly described our mortal challenges).

Think of this: At the very time I needed the unique power available to me in the temple, I didn't go to the temple!

I was too busy, too lazy, too preoccupied with "good" things to go to the very place I needed to go: the powerhouse of the Lord! The temple!

However, before our friend's truck drove away—packed to the hilt with more than seventy boxes of "stuff" all safely secured with tarps and ropes and bungee cords—I had figured out a plan to be in the temple for multiple experiences on three days in a row. It would start with being with my husband when he would seal a bride and groom. I determined that following the sealing, I would go directly to an endowment session.

I was desperate to be safely inside the temple and to stay there. I was so ready for personal revelation.

For comfort. For peace: the kind of peace found *only* within the walls of the temple. I was ready to learn— to be taught by the Spirit in the Lord's house.

I followed through on my plan. I attended the temple sealing and then hurried to an endowment session. As I did so, a most remarkable, never-to-be-forgotten moment happened. *As soon as* I sat down in the endowment room, I had a very clear impression, one that signaled that my focus during the preceding few weeks indeed had left something to be desired. This impression came in the form of a rebuke.

My first reaction was to doubt that I had really understood that impression. Surely heaven wasn't displeased with me—not after all of that good work I had just completed. I was tempted to counter that impression with: *Really? Have you seen our garage? Have you seen how happy my husband is?*

I had gone to the temple anticipating some pure, anchoring, restorative personal revelation, and *lots* of comfort.

I *never* anticipated chastisement.

Through the years, though, I have come to real-ize that when I have impressions expressed in a way much different from the way I express myself, I need to pay attention. The impression I received in the temple that day was phrased much differently than

I would have said it, so I knew I needed to take it seriously.

I've also learned that if I can vividly remember where I was when I heard or felt a spiritual impression, that is likely an indication that the Holy Ghost is carrying that particular message to me.

And, as was the case that morning, if chastisement is involved, I can be fairly certain that the message is from the Lord and not just my own ideas.

Also, if the message I'm receiving is consistent with truths revealed in the scriptures and by living prophets, I feel I can trust it.

That day in the temple, the message I received was puzzling, even confusing. I had found *such* a sense of accomplishment in cleaning up our garage, and even more joy in my husband's reaction. I was so happy establishing a house of order and cleanliness and finally tossing out things I wasn't using. So what was I to make of the rebuke I received as I sat down in the endowment room?

As I began to sort through my confusion, I noted to myself that even though I had planned and committed to the Lord that I was going to have four temple experiences in the next three days, that didn't stop the Spirit from conveying that chastening message to me.

What was this all about? What did I need to learn?

For almost two weeks this conundrum puzzled me. On Saturday, August 14, 2010, I was getting ready to speak at an adult stake conference session with my husband. The words *weightier matters* kept coming to my mind, but I had no time to stop preparing, so I called a friend and said, "Please go to your scripture app and do a search for 'weightier matters' and tell me what comes up."

Up came the answer to my dilemma: a verse of scripture that begins with "Woe." Now, when I hear "Woe" in the scriptures, and it feels quite personal, I can be pretty sure that I am going to be offered a little corrective feedback. I will be invited to grow. Maybe even grow up! And that was the case with the scripture passage my friend found:

"Woe unto you, scribes and Pharisees, hypocrites! for ye pay tithe of mint and anise and cummin, and have omitted the weightier matters of the law, judgment, mercy, and faith: these ought ye to have done, and not to leave the other undone" (Matthew 23:23).

There was my answer. And the way the words lodged in my heart that day was this:

"Woe unto you, Wendy!

"For you dejunked your garage and tossed out thirty

years of files that were no longer relevant to your life, but ye omitted the weightier matters of temple service and temple worship:

"These ought ye to have done, and not to leave the other undone."

That was my wake-up call!

Wake up, Wendy, to what is really important. Wake up to the weightier matters. Wake up to not leaving those weightier matters undone.

Wake up to the fact that you can do the weightier matters and still have time for those other things that you want and need to do.

Our focus matters to the Lord. It matters because our lives are a stewardship, and each day counts. As we heed our own personal wake-up calls and stop neglecting the "weightier matters," we will experience the joy of having the heavens open to us, allowing us to receive counsel to guide our lives.

CHAPTER 3

DECLARE WHAT YOU KNOW TO BE TRUE

My husband is a man who can quickly cut to the heart of an issue. He is a man who can think on his feet. Perhaps this comes from his working for thirty years as a surgeon—most of those years as an internationally renowned cardiac surgeon.

One sentence from him can change things, introduce new knowledge, soften hearts, and raise sights. For example, when he was in the midst of the unprecedented, grueling assignment to open the countries of Eastern Europe for the preaching of the gospel, he most often had only seconds to make a statement or ask a question that would keep the door of a hostile government official open long enough to commence a bridging conversation.

Personally, I can testify that his questions can be

very powerful. It was one question from him—"Will you marry me?"—that turned my life upside down. (Or, as he likes to say, "I turned your life right side up!")

When any of us are asked a question, we have about two seconds to commence our response and apparently less than eight seconds to give our full answer. A recent study from Microsoft Corporation shows that people now—because of the highly digitized world in which we live—lose their concentration after eight seconds, which is one second less than "the notoriously ill-focused goldfish."[9] Well, that may or may not be true. But the time we have to respond to a question about the Church and our beliefs is brief.

At this point in the history of the Church, we are each going to be asked questions about the Church, our standards, and our doctrine. Some of these questions will come from earnest seekers. Some will be asked by nefarious individuals who hope to undermine our faith.

It doesn't matter what the intent of a question is—we can learn how to give a useful answer. Think of the words of Peter: "Be ready *always* to give an answer to every man that asketh you a reason of the hope that is in you" (1 Peter 3:15; emphasis added).

My husband had an experience many years ago that demonstrated his capacity to be ready as Peter counseled. One day, he was asked by a medical colleague, "Why are you different from other surgeons?"

My husband's quick response was, "Well, if I am different from other surgeons, it is because I know the Book of Mormon is true!"

I've thought about my husband's remarkable answer for years now. His quick response demonstrated several things—including how missionary-minded he was as a young man and how anchored he was in the gospel of Jesus Christ. It revealed what mattered most to him.

I've thought about how my husband's statement *could very well be* the answer to so many questions people may ask us as members of The Church of Jesus Christ of Latter-day Saints, and could lead to a fruitful discussion. Consider the following:

- Why don't you do drugs or drink alcohol?
Because I know the Book of Mormon is true!

- Why do you go along with the curfew your parents set for you?
Because I know the Book of Mormon is true!

- Why don't you support so many politically correct decisions in the world?
Because I know the Book of Mormon is true!

- Why do you give 10 percent of your income to your Church when there are so many things you could buy with that money?

Because I know the Book of Mormon is true!

- Why do you go so regularly to the temple? It seems like you've stopped doing many of the things you used to like to do for entertainment and recreation—just so that you can be in the temple. Why do you do that?

Because I know the Book of Mormon is true!

- Why are you always so careful—even hypervigilant—about the websites you visit on the internet, the TV shows and movies you watch, and the music you listen to?

Because I know the Book of Mormon is true!

- Why do you regularly spend time on family history websites looking for dates and places and information about your ancestors?

Because I know the Book of Mormon is true!

- Why do you invite friends who are not of your faith into your home when you have the missionaries over for dinner?

Because I know the Book of Mormon is true!

- Why are you so willing to help others—even those who are not members of your Church?

Because I know the Book of Mormon is true!

- Why do you work so hard on those assignments that your bishop or stake president gives you?

Because I know the Book of Mormon is true!

- Why are you so weird?

Because I know the Book of Mormon is true!

(I once heard a prominent Latter-day Saint athlete tell a congregation of young single adults, "If you aren't called 'weird' at least once a day, you are not living your religion!")

Perhaps you can talk with your family members and friends about other questions you could be asked for which President Nelson's answer could be a useful response. Talk about how this simple answer could open up a rewarding conversation.

As for myself, I *do* know the Book of Mormon is true.

It is the word of God.

I've read it quickly—meaning, in a very short period of time.

I've read it slowly—one or two chapters each morning over breakfast with my husband.

I've studied it with the help of study guides and by topic, for teaching lessons and for clarifying doctrine for myself.

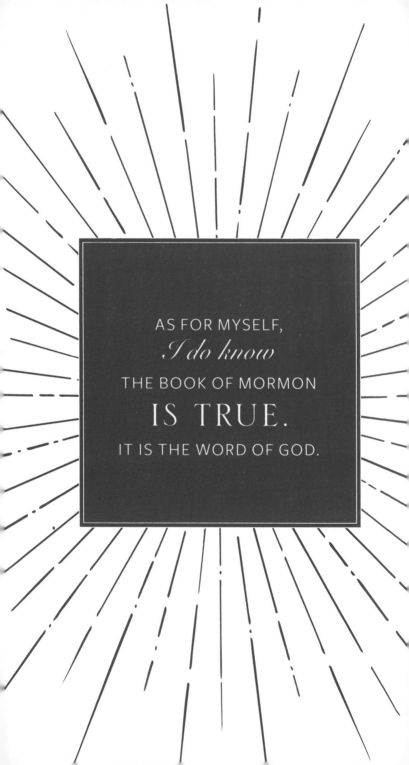

AS FOR MYSELF,
I do know
THE BOOK OF MORMON
IS TRUE.
IT IS THE WORD OF GOD.

I've listened to it, savoring the truths of a few verses, as I have drifted off to sleep.

I've also listened to it, being invigorated by the accounts in several chapters, as I get ready in the morning, or when making a meal, or when cleaning up in our kitchen.

And daily, for decades now, I've prayerfully taken a question that has been on my heart to its pages. As I have read with the Spirit with me, I have most often found the answer from the Lord that was written especially for me for that very day.

Because I know the Book of Mormon is true, I know that Joseph Smith was, and is, a true prophet—*the* Prophet of this last gospel dispensation before the Savior returns to the earth.

Because I know the Book of Mormon is true, I know that Jesus is the Christ, and I know that His infinite Atonement is real—which means the Savior will cleanse and heal us, strengthen and magnify us so that we can do *really impossible* things that the Lord needs us to do. Impossible things we never imagined.

Because I know the Book of Mormon is true, I know that The Church of Jesus Christ of Latter-day Saints is *His* Church, and that He, the Savior of this world and countless others, leads and guides His prophets, seers, and revelators on the earth today.

And *because I know the Book of Mormon is true, I know that serious, ongoing study of its pages is key to having the heavens open for us.*

CHAPTER 4

DO THINGS THE LORD'S WAY, NOT THE WORLD'S

One Sabbath day, we had the joy of attending our home ward, where, after renewing our covenants with the Lord, we were taught by a twelve-year-old boy. He told us that during the past several weeks he had become very concerned about his spiritual development.

I don't think I had ever heard a twelve-year-old express concern about his or her spiritual development! But this great young man was concerned. He told his father—who directed him to a particular general conference talk that led this boy to pray differently and to listen in a different way for the promptings of the Spirit. He was led to the principle of charity, a principle he was now exploring and implementing in his life.

This young man, along with many others whom I have met, has learned an important lesson about working in the Lord's way. The Lord's ways are different from ours. In these marvelous days, days filled to overflowing with the fulfillment of prophecies, we don't have time for things that don't really matter. We only have time for understanding truth and for doing that which we came to earth to do. In order to accomplish this, we need to do things the Lord's way.

Let me describe three situations that illustrate the principle of acting as the Lord directs and not acting after the manner of men.

Situation One

Nephi is one of my heroes—for all kinds of reasons. His impeccable obedience is always inspiring to me. Nephi was asked by the Lord to do really impossible things. (I can relate to that, and I'm sure you can as well.)

Over and over again, the Lord asked Nephi to do things Nephi simply did *not* know how to do! And yet Nephi's response was always the same. In essence, Nephi said: "I will go and do *whatever* the Lord asks me to do—not because it will be fun, or easy, or because everyone else is doing it, but because I know the Lord will show me how to do it" (see 1 Nephi 3:7).

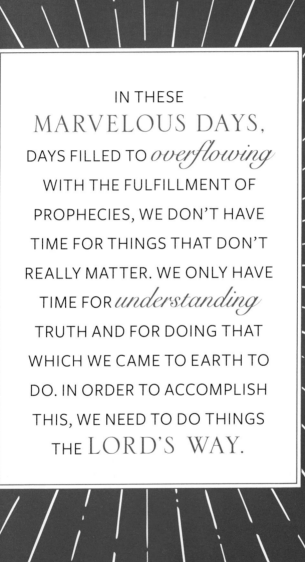

IN THESE MARVELOUS DAYS, DAYS FILLED TO *overflowing* WITH THE FULFILLMENT OF PROPHECIES, WE DON'T HAVE TIME FOR THINGS THAT DON'T REALLY MATTER. WE ONLY HAVE TIME FOR *understanding* TRUTH AND FOR DOING THAT WHICH WE CAME TO EARTH TO DO. IN ORDER TO ACCOMPLISH THIS, WE NEED TO DO THINGS THE LORD'S WAY.

At one point, the Lord told Nephi to build a ship. Nephi had no idea how to build a ship.

But the Lord gave Nephi courage when He said, "Thou shalt construct a ship, *after the manner which I shall show thee*" (1 Nephi 17:8; emphasis added).

And Nephi did! He built that ship *exactly* as the Lord directed.

Here is what Nephi said: "Now I, Nephi, did *not* work the timbers after the manner which was learned by men, neither did I build the ship after the manner of men; but I did build it after the manner which the Lord had shown unto me; wherefore, it was not after the manner of men" (1 Nephi 18:2; emphasis added).

Situation Two

The Prophet Joseph Smith was asked by the Lord to build a temple in Nauvoo. The Lord showed him exactly what the temple should look like, and William Weeks was assigned to be the temple architect.

Consider this historical account of an interchange between the Prophet and the architect:

"In February 1844, the Prophet called on William Weeks, temple architect. [On the architectural drawings,] Joseph Smith noticed semi-circular windows in the half stories separating the upper and lower halls. The Prophet politely instructed Weeks that the windows should be completely circular.

Weeks protested, stating that circular windows 'were a violation of all the known rules of architecture.'"

But because the Lord had shown the Prophet the Nauvoo Temple in vision, Joseph Smith was undaunted. He was determined that the temple would have circular windows as shown him by the Lord. The Prophet knew that the Lord was the true architect of His holy house, and so he responded to William Weeks's professional opinion accordingly: "I wish you to carry out my designs. *I have seen in vision* the splendid appearance of that building . . . and will have it built according to the pattern shown to me."[10]

If you look at a picture of the original 1846 Nauvoo Temple, you will notice the circular windows as shown in vision to the Prophet Joseph Smith.

And if you look at a picture of the rebuilt Nauvoo Temple, dedicated in 2002, you will again notice the circular windows that the Lord designed.

Situation Three

Once upon a time there was a young medical doctor by the name of Dr. Russell M. Nelson. Over the years, young Dr. Nelson became an internationally renowned cardiac surgeon.

How did he do that? Clearly there were many contributing factors. He studied hard, spent countless hours in the lab with various research teams, and learned everything he could from various mentors along the way. But one could argue that he would never have acquired the knowledge and skill he did had it not been for his willingness to seek heaven's help in his profession and at times follow the counsel of the Lord rather than the counsel of men. In fact, to become the successful surgeon he was to become—and in some instances to do what had *never* been done before—he actually had to defy the very books from which he studied.

One of his textbooks in medical school read, "Do not touch the beating heart," and went on to declare that "if you do, it will stop beating." Further, one of the most famous surgeons at that time proclaimed that *any* surgeon who would attempt to operate on the heart would lose credibility within the medical profession.

But young Dr. Nelson had a source he honored more than famous surgeons, and a book that he honored more than his medical textbooks. Dr. Nelson's source was the Lord, and the book was the Doctrine and Covenants.

Early in his career, Dr. Nelson came across two truths articulated in the Doctrine and Covenants that opened his mind and heart to further inspiration. These truths were: first, that all blessings are predicated upon obedience to divine law (see Doctrine and Covenants 130:21), and second, that to *every* kingdom there is a law given (see Doctrine and Covenants 88:38).

These doctrinal verities led Dr. Nelson to ask himself, "What are the eternal laws that govern the beating heart?" That question opened up further insights and inspiration that allowed him to help, alongside others, pioneer open-heart surgery.

One accomplishment led to another, and Dr. Nelson was soon recognized as one of the acknowledged pioneers and leaders in his field. He received awards and honorary doctorates from educational institutions and was invited to be a visiting professor in many countries.

Then, at the height of his professional career, on April 6, 1984, Dr. Nelson was summoned to Church headquarters, where President Gordon B. Hinckley, then a counselor to President Spencer W. Kimball, extended the call from the Lord that had come to President Kimball for Dr. Nelson to serve as a member of the Quorum of the Twelve Apostles. As in the days of the early Apostles, when most were called away from their fishing nets and other fields of labor, Dr. Nelson was called to step out of the operating room and go forth into the world as a special witness of the Lord Jesus Christ. He was called to preach the gospel of Jesus Christ to every nation, kindred, tongue, and people so that the Savior Himself could open the heart, soften the heart, heal the heart, and change the heart of every person who would choose to follow Him.

Many professional colleagues were dumbfounded that a man of his experience and recognition would lay his esteemed career aside. Fellow surgeons and nurses with whom he had worked were perplexed at this sudden change of course in his life. Did Dr. Nelson realize what he was doing? Didn't he realize that he had patients, students, and colleagues around the world depending on him? How could he possibly leave them?

Dr. Nelson was able to change the course of his life, just as each Apostle who had preceded him, because he had long since consecrated himself to the Lord. A prophet of God had extended this call, and in the very moment, his focus shifted entirely to the work of the Lord.

Our experiences may not be as dramatic as building a ship, or a temple, or a heart-lung machine, but true followers of Jesus Christ can expect certain things to happen during the course of their lives:

First, as a true disciple, you will have times when

it will not seem logical to follow a certain course of action that you feel prompted to follow. What you are drawn to do—even feel compelled to do—will fly in the face of all mortal knowledge and wisdom. And yet, you will know you are to do it because *it is of God.*

Second, as a true follower, you will face times when you won't have a clue about how to proceed with what you feel the Lord wants you to do. Like you, I know how both of these things feel.

What do we do in such circumstances?

Do exactly what the Lord has told you and will tell you to do. Follow with *exactness* His directions. The Lord *will* provide the way! Step by step.

If you truly want to fill the measure of your creation, follow the examples of other men and women who, as true followers of Jesus Christ, have been willing to do *whatever* the Lord asks them to do. The challenge is to be like Nephi, and Joseph Smith, and President Nelson, and live your life *not after the manner of men.*

This principle holds true in all aspects of our lives. As you build your marriage, build it *not* after the manner of men. Pray to know how the Lord would have you and your spouse strengthen your marriage. You will then co-create a marriage with

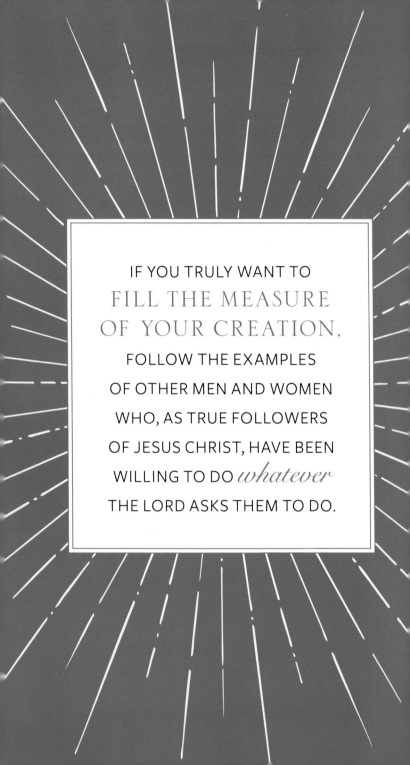

IF YOU TRULY WANT TO
FILL THE MEASURE
OF YOUR CREATION,
FOLLOW THE EXAMPLES
OF OTHER MEN AND WOMEN
WHO, AS TRUE FOLLOWERS
OF JESUS CHRIST, HAVE BEEN
WILLING TO DO *whatever*
THE LORD ASKS THEM TO DO.

your spouse and the Lord that will bring comfort, joy, and love to you and your spouse all the days of your life, no matter what is happening around you. You will have a marriage on earth that will prepare you for eternal life together.

Likewise, as you
- build your family,
- build your relationships,
- build your career, and
- help to build up Zion,

do not build after the manner of men. Lay those mortal plans aside. Build according to how the Lord will show you.

The heavens will open as the Lord knows that you are sincere in following *with exactness His* plans, *His* instructions. And you will find great joy and great success in this life and in the life to come.

CHAPTER 5

HEED WARNING SIGNS

I'm intrigued with signs and particularly some of the unique signs we come upon as we travel. My husband knows this and has often pulled off to the side of the road so I could snap a photo. One such sign in Brazil near a beach read: "Swimmers have an increased likelihood of being attacked by a shark!" Apparently even with that sign posted, swimmers *still* go into the ocean in that area—and, as the sign warns, they are still attacked by sharks!

In a similar fashion, the Lord through His prophets posts many signs along the path of our mortal journey. Sometimes the evidence that the heavens are open comes through prophetic pronouncements and spiritual promptings we receive of what *not* to do. Warnings.

I learned this truth as a young single adult. I was twenty-four years old, attending graduate school at Brigham Young University, and engaged to be married.

I received my temple endowment a couple of months prior to our wedding date and then began to attend regularly. During subsequent visits to the temple, I began to wonder if I should really marry this man. And that uncertainty only increased.

As April general conference of that year approached, my bishop said from the pulpit one Sunday, "If you have a problem or a question, take it to general conference, and you will get it answered."

My bishop did not know that I was engaged, but it felt like he was talking directly to me, just letting the rest of the congregation listen in. I *did* have a question, so I determined to do just as my bishop had counseled. I would take it to general conference.

On Saturday of that April conference, my roommate had a major paper to write. She was off to the library, so, gratefully, I was home alone. Because I was desperate for an answer to this growing dilemma, I watched general conference in a spirit of fasting and prayer.

I was recording that conference on audiotapes for

my family in Canada, so as conference began, I hit the "record" button.

Then something unusual happened. As I prayerfully listened with the question in my heart, "Should I marry this man?" every talk—*every single talk*—was on the subject of *marriage!*

Yet the message I received at the end of that day of conference was clear: *"Do not marry this man."*

As general conference concluded, I turned off the recorder and the TV, walked to the kitchen where the yellow phone hung on the wall, called my fiancé, who was not living in Utah, and ended our engagement.

He was not cheerful, and neither were his family members and friends. Over the next few days, I received phone calls from those interested in our relationship. They would point out this man's many great qualities, and, attempting to be gentle and discreet—and failing at both—some asked: "Wendy, do you know that you are twenty-four years old?" (implying—well, we know what they were implying).

Actually, I hadn't lost my mind or my birth certificate. I knew exactly how old I was. And I also knew what I had heard in my mind and in my heart. I had heard the words: "Do not marry this man." And I could not—and would not—deny that.

Life went on. He married shortly thereafter, and he and his wife had three children. I was happy for them. I had no bad feelings toward them. I only knew what I had heard. We went our separate ways, and I followed promptings from heaven to continue my education.

Several years later, I received a thick envelope in the mail and immediately recognized the beautiful handwriting on the outside. The letter was from my former fiancé. I anticipated that he was going to tell me about all the wonderful things happening in their family's life.

Instead, that letter was one of the most heart-wrenching communications I have ever received. My friend wrote me of the heartache that was coming to their family. He and his wife were divorcing because he was choosing a path apart from the gospel-centered one they had started out on.

How grateful I was for the counsel I had received from the Lord through the whisperings of the Holy Ghost as I watched that general conference!

Now, there is an interesting postscript to this story. A few weeks after I received that letter, I was asked to teach a lesson on marriage in my ward Relief Society. For the lesson, I wanted to bring in some of the words of the Brethren, and I remembered those well-labeled audiotapes from that April general conference in which *every* talk was on marriage.

I found the tapes and started listening.

This experience was startlingly different from the first. Not one talk was on marriage. *Not one!* And no one said, "Do not marry this man." But that was exactly what I had heard.

I marvel at the Lord's loving kindness. He not only had the Holy Ghost deliver that message and tender mercy to me, but He also refrained from adding: "Oh, and by the way, Wendy, it will be *more than thirty years* before your husband shows up!"

My experience of heeding the Lord's warning to me taught me the importance of heeding other warnings, some on signs. Perhaps you've seen on a piece of clothing the sign: "One size fits all." Some people read this sign as a warning: "This doesn't look that great on anyone!" But as I've considered it, I can see how that sign, *One size fits all,* actually can apply to how the Spirit teaches us.

One size really can fit all when it comes to receiving personal revelation. By this I mean that *whatever* is said over the pulpit, in a class, in the temple, or in any learning situation can fit each one of us perfectly—because the Holy Ghost can *tailor-make* whatever is offered to *fit each person exactly*! That is what happened to me in that long-ago general conference, and it has happened more times than I can count in the years since then.

I love the words of Elder Richard G. Scott: "The Lord will not force you to learn. You must exercise your agency to authorize the Spirit to teach you."[11]

I don't know what you need to learn, but the Lord does. The Holy Ghost is the true teacher, and as you *exercise your agency to authorize Him* to teach you, the heavens will open and He will bring you the message the Lord wants *you* to hear *now*.

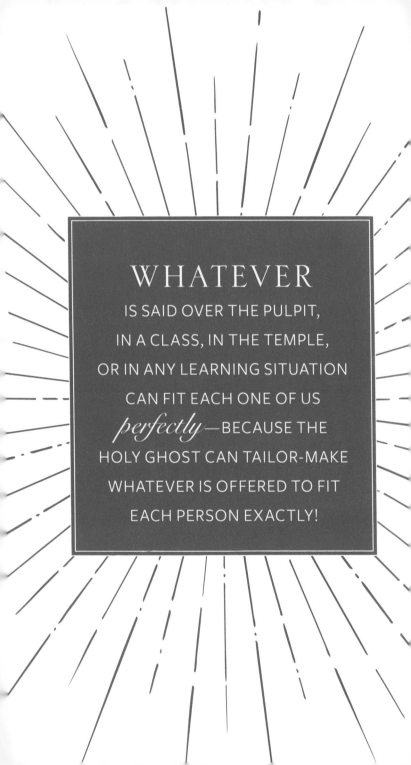

WHATEVER
IS SAID OVER THE PULPIT,
IN A CLASS, IN THE TEMPLE,
OR IN ANY LEARNING SITUATION
CAN FIT EACH ONE OF US
perfectly—BECAUSE THE
HOLY GHOST CAN TAILOR-MAKE
WHATEVER IS OFFERED TO FIT
EACH PERSON EXACTLY!

CHAPTER 6

SEARCH DILIGENTLY
IN THE LIGHT OF CHRIST

When I was growing up, I read and studied in a variety of places in our home. It didn't matter whether I was in the front room, at the kitchen table, or on my bed, my mother would always find me and say, "Would you like a little more light on the subject?" Actually, I wanted a *lot* more light on the subject! I needed increased illumination—of the pages, of my mind, and of the topic.

Mom would then proceed to turn on another light. Her consistent interest and comforting presence would tell me that even the seemingly impossible task before me *was* possible—that with continuing effort on my part and the increased light she had provided, I would succeed.

Do you need more light on a subject? Could you

use an increased illumination of your mind—more light in your life?

What kind of light do you need? What kind of light would help you the most these days?

- a healing light
- a comforting light
- a warming light
- a calming light
- a reverent light

Or would you prefer

- a clarifying light
- a revealing light
- a hope-filled light

Or is the help you need to be found in

- an invigorating light
- an inspiring light
- a beckoning light

How about

- a heart-changing light
- a mind-stretching light
- a soul-stirring light

Or do you need

- a hand-holding light
- an embracing light
- a kindly light

Or are you increasingly looking for

- a refining light
- a hallowing light
- a sanctifying light

Or do you find yourself saying, "I need all of the above, please"?

The good news is that the Light of Jesus Christ is all of these kinds of light . . . and so much more.

However, some of us seem to be satisfied with or drawn to lesser lights. The light of the refrigerator seems to captivate many of us. Or maybe we feel the pull of the light from the computer or the light from the TV or the light from our smartphone or tablet. We may even be captivated by what we believe is the limelight.

Have you a light in your life that compels you and that seems to propel your life *more* than the Light of Christ does? Is there a distracting light in your life that blinds you to the possibilities that could be yours if you were to access more light from the true Source of all true light?

The Savior Jesus Christ is the Source of all true light. He is the master of eternal light. He is the Light of the World. And He has given His light, the Light of Christ, the light of truth, to everyone. It is a free gift, a glorious divine inheritance that allows each person to distinguish good from evil.

Think of this: Without the Light and the Laws of Jesus Christ, all nature would wither, all vision would disappear, the stars would fall out of alignment, our ability to know good from evil would be obliterated—and God would not be able to communicate with us. And, the heavens could *never* be open to us.

Elder Bruce R. McConkie explained that the Light of Christ "is the instrumentality and agency by which Deity keeps in touch and communes with all his children, both the righteous and the wicked." Doesn't that sound like a great summoning and homing device? Further, he said, the Light of Christ "has an edifying, enlightening, and uplifting influence on men [and women]. One of its manifestations is called conscience, through which all men [and women] know right from wrong."

Elder McConkie continued: "[The Light of Christ] is the means by which the Lord invites and entices all . . . to improve their lot and to come unto him and receive his gospel."[12]

When you read in the scriptures that the Light of Christ is in the sun, and in the moon, and in the stars, and in the earth (see Doctrine and Covenants

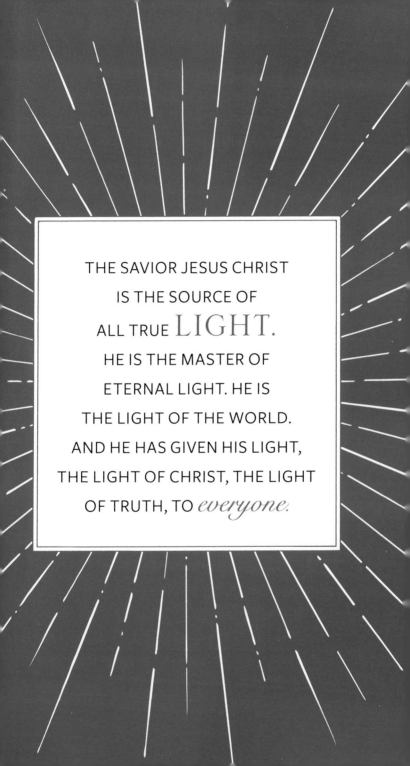

THE SAVIOR JESUS CHRIST
IS THE SOURCE OF
ALL TRUE LIGHT.
HE IS THE MASTER OF
ETERNAL LIGHT. HE IS
THE LIGHT OF THE WORLD.
AND HE HAS GIVEN HIS LIGHT,
THE LIGHT OF CHRIST, THE LIGHT
OF TRUTH, TO *everyone.*

88:7–13), does that not stir your soul, entreating you to want to understand more? And when you catch even a *glimpse* of what it might mean that His Light, the Light of Christ, gives light to your eyes and quickens your understanding, does that not uplift, amaze, and humble you all in the same sparkling moment?

When you need more light in your life, consider reading, pondering, and praying about section 88 of the Doctrine and Covenants, and see what happens. You know those times as you're reading the scriptures when you feel yourself getting close to something more wonderful than you've uncovered or discovered before, and you don't want to breathe for fear of dislodging the increasing light? The 88th section gives me that "I-don't-dare-breathe" kind of feeling. It is one of my light-filled scriptural oases. I can never study it enough.

The Lord loves to teach us about light—which then *adds* to our light. He says, "That which is of God is light; and he that receiveth light, and continueth in God, receiveth more light" (Doctrine and Covenants 50:24).

Do you see how generous the Lord is? He gives us the Light of Christ, which guides us to even *more* light! Do you think *He* loves light? And do you think

He loves us? And do you think He desires for us to love light and to be lifted, enlightened, and loved and have the kind of light, love, and life that He has?

Would you like a little more light on the subject of the Light of Jesus Christ? Truman G. Madsen sheds some. He said, "We have light that enables us to see *objects* here, but the Light of Jesus Christ lights the *subject*. It illumines minds and spirits—yes, and bodies."[13]

This is possible because of the following promise from the Lord: "And if your eye be single to my glory, your whole bodies shall be filled with light, and there shall be no darkness in you; and that body which is filled with light comprehendeth all things" (Doctrine and Covenants 88:67; see also Luke 11:34–36).

So, how can we obtain more light in our lives?

Remember Mahonri Moriancumr, the brother of Jared? When he needed to find a way to put light into the unusual vessels the Lord had directed him to build, he took his request to the Lord. The Lord responded by asking, "What will ye that *I* should do?" (Ether 2:23; emphasis added) and then basically taught the "study-it-out-in-*your*-mind-and-then-get-back-to-me" principle.

That particular principle is a vital key for each of us. If we don't work, putting forth effort to study out the situations for which we need more light, we'll *never* receive more light, because we will never have a specific plan to offer to the Lord. As President Nelson often says, "The Lord likes effort."

As the brother of Jared followed the prescribed process, which involved faith in every footstep, the culminating enlightening moment was *not* when the Lord touched the well-prepared sixteen stones. Rather, it was when the brother of Jared *saw* the spirit body of the Lord. Mahonri Moriancumr received *more light* than he asked for or than he had ever imagined.

As the Lord expressed it, "Never have I showed myself unto man whom I have created, for never has man believed in me as thou hast" (Ether 3:15). The brother of Jared's *faith* had invited full visual disclosure of the Lord.

The Lord has a great desire to give us *all* the light we are ready to receive—and all the light that our faith can draw forth. But it requires consistent effort on our part, a dedicated demonstration of our faith through diligent searching.

The prophet Mormon pleaded, "I beseech of you, . . . that ye should search diligently in the light of Christ that ye may know good from evil; and if ye will lay hold upon every good thing, and condemn

THE LORD HAS A
GREAT DESIRE TO GIVE US
ALL THE LIGHT WE ARE
READY TO RECEIVE—
AND ALL THE LIGHT THAT OUR
faith CAN DRAW FORTH.
BUT IT REQUIRES CONSISTENT
effort ON OUR PART,
A DEDICATED DEMONSTRATION
OF OUR FAITH THROUGH
diligent searching.

it not, ye certainly will be a child of Christ" (Moroni 7:19).

In this admonition from Mormon, I hear his reference to Isaiah's wisdom about these last days—our days—in which some people do indeed "call evil good, and good evil," and some "put darkness for light, and light for darkness," and some "put bitter for sweet, and sweet for bitter" (Isaiah 5:20; 2 Nephi 15:20).

The ability to distinguish good from evil, light from darkness is soul-threateningly important. Today, far too many who are *not* heeding the light of Christ appallingly call physical, emotional, and even sexual abuse "love." Others mistakenly call the freedom that comes through choosing to keep the Lord's commandments "confining." Some unwisely call the prophets "men without vision"; others call wickedness "a right" and consider repentance to be "a quick fix" or "permission to break our covenants."

Maybe you're thinking: "Good from evil? That's not a problem for me! I'm trying to figure out better from best these days."[14] However, there may be other distinctions that need to be discerned in your life—distinctions between activities that *invite* more light into your life and those that *dispel* the light that is already there. Your personal spiritual wattage will be increased or diminished accordingly.

Discerning may involve such questions as these:

- Should I gratify what the world tells me are my "needs" or fill the measure of my creation?
- Is a new, time-consuming, exciting project in my life one more step forward in fulfilling the mission for which I was sent to earth, or is it really just a distraction, constituting one giant step backward or sideways?
- In my relationships, do I distinguish what is worth speaking up about from that which is worth keeping quiet about? And when I do speak up, do others experience my voice as one of repetitive encouragement or as nagging?

As we search diligently in the Light of Christ, we can find answers to these questions that are more important than we may have ever realized.

In the scriptures we are entreated to

- trust *in* Christ (Moroni 9:22),
- be faithful *in* Christ (Moroni 9:25),
- be perfected *in* Him (Moroni 10:32),
- pray *in* His name (3 Nephi 18:19),
- be alive *in* Christ (2 Nephi 25:25),
- have faith *in* his name (Moroni 7:26),

- walk *in* the light of the Lord (2 Nephi 12:5), and again, from Mormon, to
- search diligently *in* the Light of Christ (Moroni 7:19).

Why didn't Mormon use the preposition *with?* It seems that searching diligently "with" the light of Christ could imply a separateness from Him—as if our searching were something external to us. What Mormon plants in our minds is an "embedded-in" reciprocity between us and the Light, Life, and Love of our Savior.

In Mormon's words, and indeed in each of the scriptural injunctions previously listed, I hear a compelling invitation to intertwine our lives with the Savior—nesting our lives *in* His power, in His light, and in His love. That means nesting our difficulties, struggles, temptations, loneliness, disappointments, sorrows, pains, and yes, also our successes and joys *in* Him. It is *within* that nesting that we will find the strength, comfort, answers, and rest for which we are so diligently, even desperately, searching.

That intertwining, and that nesting, will open the heavens for us.

CHAPTER 7

LAY HOLD UPON
EVERY GOOD THING

After inviting us to search *in* the light of Christ that we may know good from evil, the prophet Mormon invites us to take the next step in having the heavens open to us. He invites us to "lay hold upon every good thing" (Moroni 7:19).

This wonderful invitation to take an active part in laying hold on the blessings our Father has in store for us comes with some caveats, however. Some people, for example, mistakenly think they need to lay hold on *every* good thing *all at once.*

The scriptures tell us that "to every thing there is a season" (Ecclesiastes 3:1). We need to add to *that* piece of wisdom the phrase: "in the Lord's due time." Hence: To everything there is a season—*in the Lord's due time.* And speaking of times, there are times that we need to "run with patience the race that is set before us" (Hebrews 12:1), but at the same time we are not supposed to "run faster than [we have] strength" (Mosiah 4:27). And there will be many times when the most important thing we need to do is to "be still, and know" that He is God (Psalm 46:10). That is when, *if* we have "cheerfully [done] all things that lie in our power," we can wait "with the utmost assurance . . . for his arm to be revealed" (Doctrine and Covenants 123:17).

What other good things can open the heavens for us?

President Ezra Taft Benson said it well: "Men and women who turn their lives over to God will discover that He can make a lot more out of their lives than they can. He will deepen their joys, expand their vision, quicken their minds, strengthen their muscles, lift their spirits, multiply their blessings, increase their opportunities, comfort their souls, raise up friends, and pour out peace."[15] Turning our lives over to God is an important way to open the heavens as He guides us to lay hold upon more good things.

Those additional good things might include inspiring words. When we recognize the power of words and use our words to build others, we are laying hold upon a good thing. The Apostle Peter speaks of the importance of words. He counsels us to "[lay] aside all malice, and all guile, and hypocrisies, and envies, and all evil speakings" (1 Peter 2:1).

Words matter. Because words lodge in our cells and in our souls and even in the walls of our homes, think of how important it is to be exquisitely mindful of our words. Think of how important it is to use words that strengthen our spirits and those of others, the temples of our bodies, and the temples of our homes. Words can bring joy and love and hope and peace into our homes and our relationships. Words can invite the Spirit. Words can allow the heavens to open for us. Words that do this are *good things.*

I have learned that one of the best ways to invite the Spirit into a home, into a relationship, or even into a congregation is to express genuine love. There is great power in three simple words spoken from our hearts: *We love you.* Or four: *The Lord loves you.*

Other four-word phrases that can miraculously open the door to other good things are: *I am so sorry,* and, *It was my fault,* and, *I do forgive you.*

Elder Jeffrey R. Holland once spoke of yet another hopeful, encouraging, peaceful word that will open the heavens faster than almost any other. He said: "The very beauty of the word *repentance* is the

WORDS

CAN BRING JOY AND LOVE
AND HOPE AND PEACE
INTO OUR HOMES AND
OUR RELATIONSHIPS.
WORDS CAN INVITE THE SPIRIT.
WORDS CAN ALLOW THE
heavens to open FOR US.

promise of escaping old problems and old habits and old sorrows and old sins. It is among the most hopeful and encouraging—and yes, most peaceful—words in the gospel vocabulary."[16]

Elder Holland's insights are so important, particularly for people who assume they are not worthy to lay hold on *any* good thing, let alone *every* good thing, because of their past sins.

This limiting view of the Savior's power to cleanse and heal us and make us whole again, as we truly repent, is promoted by the adversary, not inspired by God. If you feel guilt and grief, that is actually a good sign—an indication of your continued goodness. Congratulate yourself on still being able to feel guilty! The light is still there!

Guilt can be a good thing. Guilt has received a lot of bad press in the past, yet guilt, if used well, is exactly the help most of us need to stop sinning. *Let* your guilt start you on the path of the sincere, heartfelt, and therefore heart-changing process of laying down your sins—giving away your sins to know the Lord (see Alma 22:18). And as you come to know Him, and come closer to Him than you ever have before, you will also come to know the real you—unshackled and free from your past!

Repentance is a good thing. The Savior and your

ecclesiastical leaders, as needed, will lead you along. The Savior really did mean it when He said, "Though your sins be as scarlet, they shall be as white as snow; though they be red like crimson, they shall be as wool" (Isaiah 1:18).

I love what the Lord says as recorded in Doctrine and Covenants 61:2: "I, the Lord, forgive sins, and am merciful unto those who confess their sins with humble hearts."

Can you hear the Savior pleading: "Please believe me. This is what I do. I forgive sins. Bring your humble heart, confess your sins, and I will extend my mercy. You do your part, and I'll do mine."

Maybe it's hard for us to believe in the Savior's forgiveness of our mistakes and sins because *we* have a hard time forgiving others. Many of us act as if forgiveness and repentance are only for the righteous. "Oh, she's a good person—I forgive her." What about those people who have caused us physical, emotional, mental, or spiritual pain and suffering? What about those who show *no* remorse that they have broken almost every commandment and have dramatically and negatively affected our lives through their choice to sin? Do we have to forgive *them?*

The Lord's instruction on this matter is quite clear: "I, the Lord, will forgive whom I will forgive, but of you it is required to forgive *all* men" (Doctrine and Covenants 64:10; emphasis added).

There are a lot of people who wish this scripture read in the reverse. They want to pick and choose whom *they* will forgive, based on their own standard of "forgive-ability." And their ultimate criterion seems to be that the sinner must suffer *more* than those who have suffered at the hands of the sinner.

Forgiveness is a good thing. So, what happens if we *don't* forgive others who have wronged us? The Lord is also clear about this outcome: "If ye forgive not men their trespasses neither will your Father forgive your trespasses" (3 Nephi 13:14–15).

Further, He tells us: "Wherefore, I say unto you, that ye ought to forgive one another; for he that forgiveth not his brother his trespasses standeth condemned before the Lord; for there remaineth in him the *greater* sin" (Doctrine and Covenants 64:9; emphasis added).

Seriously? Yes.

The Lord has set a great example for us to say what we mean and mean what we say.

Here is the reality that most of us have experienced: *unforgiveness ultimately leads to increased suffering.* How can we lay hold upon *good* things when *hard* feelings are lodged in our minds and hearts, wreaking havoc and actually causing *more* mental, emotional, physical, and spiritual pain and agony than the initial sin caused? When the Lord commands us to forgive, it is for *our own* well-being. His concern is for *us*. He wants *us* to be free from the pain and bitterness and anger that tend to linger in an unforgiving heart.

Forgiving is not easy, nor is it something that happens overnight, but it *is* possible—or the Lord would not have asked us to do it. He has commanded us to forgive others, so we need to find a way. And He will help us if we ask Him. Just like Nephi, we can say, "I *will* go and do the things [*like forgive the one who hurt me so much*] which the Lord hath commanded" (1 Nephi 3:7; emphasis added). That scripture can give us the courage to discover with the help of the Lord how to be free—gloriously free, once and for all—from the shackles of unforgiveness!

In conversations with the Lord, with caring people you trust, and perhaps with the one who harmed you—with witnesses present—healing can happen. But pay special attention to the counsel of Elder Jeffrey R. Holland: "[The Savior] did *not* say, . . . 'In order to forgive fully, you have to reenter a toxic relationship or return to an abusive, destructive circumstance.'"[17]

WHEN THE LORD COMMANDS
US TO FORGIVE,
IT IS FOR *our own* WELL-BEING.
HIS CONCERN IS FOR *us.*
HE WANTS *us* TO BE FREE FROM
THE PAIN AND BITTERNESS AND
ANGER THAT TEND TO LINGER
IN AN *unforgiving heart.*

As you pray to forgive your perpetrator, the power of Jesus Christ will heal you. His Atonement is the best thing!—not just a "good thing." It is the most glorious thing. It is that which allows us to lay hold upon *every good thing*—no matter what has happened in our past.

I'm captivated with Mormon's challenge to *lay hold upon* every good thing. When we "lay hold upon" something, it becomes real to us. There is an implied permanence, a focusing, an embracing, and a making something our own.

Conversely, what happens when we find a good thing but just deal with it lightly?

What is the impact over time on our lives of superficially reading the scriptures?

What is the impact of a tenuous testimony?

What is the impact of service done to be seen of others?

What happens when we join the Church in the same way some of us join a gym—only to show up sporadically, mainly for social reasons, but without any sense of real membership, commitment, involvement, or a desire to really work out?

What happens when year after year we do not *lay hold upon* good things but we continue to only touch good things lightly? What happens then? We may find that we are crying. But not unto the Lord. We may find that we are not losing our lives in His service and for His sake and thus finding our lives (see Matthew 10:39). Rather, we may find that we are just losing our lives, losing our hearts' former desires, and losing our stamina and interest in good things. And some days it may seem like we are losing our minds. Discouragement and despondency may set in, and we may wonder what is wrong when we are "doing everything right."

We're doing good things, aren't we?

But if we are doing good things *without* depth of feeling, without passion, without deep love, without vigor and commitment, without intentional consistency, without *laying hold upon* the good things, we will miss out on the joy. And all the joy that comes from laying hold upon good things will continually elude our feeble, flimsy grasp.

When we don't *lay hold upon* good things, we may begin to move from "touching good things lightly" to "playing around with good things" to "taking for granted good things" to even "making fun of good things."

Thus, Mormon's counsel is rivetingly true: *Lay hold upon* every good thing—especially if we want the heavens to open for us.

Now, what are the good things we want to lay hold upon?

- Better family relationships?
- A greater understanding of the scriptures?
- More peace in our lives?

How about *every good thing* that is mentioned in the hymn "More Holiness Give Me"? What difference would you notice in your life if you were to lay hold upon:

More holiness?

More strivings within? (that is, more sincere efforts)

More patience in suffering?

More sorrow for sin?

More faith in your Savior?

More sense of His care?

More joy in His service?

More purpose in prayer?[18]

There are many more good things mentioned in this beautiful hymn, including gratitude, trust, hope, meekness, purity, and strength. But the great desire is expressed in the final line, "More, Savior, like thee."

If we have foremost in our hearts a yearning to be just a little more like Jesus Christ every day, we will naturally have a longing to *lay hold upon* every good thing. Today is the day for us to do soul-stretching, marvelous things we've never done before. Persistent mighty prayer will give us access to the Savior's atoning power, and we will increasingly see as He sees, love as He loves, and become His own. In other words, the heavens will increasingly open for us.

CHAPTER 8

TAKE A QUESTION TO
GENERAL CONFERENCE

One late Friday afternoon on the first weekend in April 1992, I headed out from my home in Calgary, Alberta, Canada, for a two-and-a-half-hour drive to be with my widowed father in my hometown of Raymond, Alberta, for the weekend. We were looking forward to enjoying general conference together.

With all the busyness and intensity of end-of-semester demands on me as a university professor, I was looking forward to the spiritual renewal of conference and the joy of taking care of my dad. I was well prepared except for one thing: *What was the one question I most needed to have answered?* I had fleetingly thought about it for several weeks but couldn't settle on anything. I didn't want to "waste" a general conference, attending without a question in my heart and mind. General conference was one of my favorite times for personal revelation.

I reviewed possible questions: I didn't need to seek revelation about whether to marry the wonderful man I had been dating. I already had my answer (and the answer was no). I didn't need to seek help about my father, who had been dying, as he was now doing remarkably well. So, what was my question?

Sometimes we pray to know what to pray about. As I prayed in that manner that night in our Raymond family home, the question that came to my mind was, "Am I doing everything I should be doing with my life?" I thought, *Hmmm. Good question. I never would have thought of that.* That was when I knew the heavens had opened to give me that question.

During the welcoming remarks of the opening session of conference on Saturday, April 4, 1992, the letters *B-Y-U* came to my mind. *BYU? What?* Those letters startled me, jogging my memory. Suddenly, I recalled that a couple of weeks earlier I had tossed out a letter from Brigham Young University announcing the opening of a professorial position in its Marriage and Family Therapy graduate programs. Because the letter had seemed like a form letter that I assumed was sent to many others, and because I

SOMETIMES
WE *pray* TO KNOW
WHAT TO *pray* ABOUT.

was very happy with my life in Calgary at work, at church, and with my friends and family, I had discarded the letter and hadn't thought about it again.

Yet there on that Saturday morning during the first few moments of general conference, *BYU* was the message that came clearly to my mind. I couldn't believe it, but I also couldn't deny it.

On Sunday evening, after general conference had concluded, I thought, *Wendy, you can't pray "lead me, guide me" and then say "just kidding" when a thought you never expected, and never wanted, comes to your mind.* So as I drove back to Calgary, I decided I would phone BYU on Monday. It would be embarrassing, as the deadline for applications for the position had been April 1. Monday would be April 6. I was certain that this was one of those moments when, like Abraham, I really didn't need to do what was asked—I just needed to *show* that I was willing.

On Monday, I called and inquired if the position had been filled. "No, but we have five or six *very fine* applicants," the person on the other end informed me.

See, I thought, *I don't really have to do this.* But I also knew I had to show the Lord that I truly was willing. So I proceeded: "I know that it's past the deadline, but is there any point in my submitting my application?"

"Oh, sure," the person on the other end yawned, exuding disinterest. And that was the end of the conversation.

Nonetheless, I gathered all the required materials, submitted my application, and then turned my full attention to the relentless demands of my teaching, research, and clinical practice at the University of Calgary. I was certain I would never hear from BYU again, but I felt I had done my part in following through with my general conference prompting.

About two weeks later, as I was packing up my car in preparation to drive my dad to Utah to attend my sister's graduation at Brigham Young University, the telephone rang. It was someone calling from BYU.

"Dr. Watson," the person said with enthusiasm, "your materials arrived, and we are very interested in talking with you further. We understand that you are coming to BYU to attend graduation in a couple of days. While you are here, we would like you to make a theory presentation and a research presentation to our faculty, and also do clinical supervision with our doctoral students."

I was stunned. "May I call you right back?" I asked.

I dropped to my knees and prayed. "Heavenly Father," I said, "I usually like to go well prepared when I make a presentation. I have no time to prepare, as I am leaving in a few minutes on this trip, but if it is important for me to make these presentations, please help me."

I called back to BYU and accepted the invitation to present. Then I quickly loaded up *every* presentation overhead transparency I could find and stuffed them all into the trunk of my car. (Those were the days long before PowerPoint presentations were nicely accessible on our iPads and iPhones!)

I can still remember the feeling of walking down the hallway at BYU to make my first presentation. I felt something I never expected: *I'm home. I'm home. I'm home.* That was *not* what I wanted to feel. As much as I had loved Brigham Young University as a master's degree candidate seventeen years earlier, I had never considered teaching there. But I couldn't deny the feeling that I was "home."

I also couldn't imagine that I would be selected as the one to fill the vacancy. But I was.

Then, reality set in. How would I maneuver through the land mines and jump the international hurdles to get from the University of Calgary in Canada to Brigham Young University in the United States of America? How could I manage the abundance of negative feelings from others about leaving my well-established life in Calgary and my twelve years as a professor at the university?

I remember walking into my kitchen trying to sort through the morass. As I did so, the following words came to my mind: *"I will open an effectual door for you."* (I can still feel the power of those words.) I wrote those unusual words in my journal. I didn't remember ever hearing the term *effectual door* before. I liked it. It wasn't until several years later that I found those words as I was studying the Doctrine and Covenants (see Doctrine and Covenants 100:3; 112:19; 118:3). How had I never seen them before? It seems impossible, but somehow in my study of the scriptures, to that point in my life, those words had never registered with me. But oh, how they registered *that* day, embedding in my memory forever even the very place I was standing when I heard them!

Well, the Lord *did* open an effectual door for me (many, actually), and on Monday, January 4, 1993, I opened the door to the John Taylor Building to commence my first day of teaching at BYU. As I stepped across the threshold, the following words came to my mind: "It's not about the job."

Seriously? It's not about the job? I've just left my home, my native land, my family, and my friends; been stripped of my professional tenure as I crossed the border; and—it's not about the job?

I walked up the stairs and down the hallway to my office, opened the door, fell to my knees, and told the Lord that if it wasn't about the job, I was willing to do *whatever* He needed me to do. And then I went to work.

I *loved* my first day of teaching graduate students at BYU. I felt the greatest degree of academic freedom I had *ever* experienced. I could teach about marriage and family therapy while braiding in gospel concepts and scriptures along the way. It was thrilling to watch keen graduate students light up as the Spirit helped me to teach and them to learn. I was in professorial heaven! At the end of that first day of teaching, I almost floated down the hall to my office, thinking, *Well, even if it's not about the job, I'm loving this!*

A note on my door interrupted my reverie. The note read: "Would you be willing to meet with Dr. Allen Bergin?" Would I? He had long been my professional hero for pioneering the blending of concepts of spirituality into the field of psychology. In fact, as I was packing boxes in Calgary, I remember thinking, "Once I have a little credibility on campus— maybe in ten years—I really would like to meet Dr. Allen Bergin. I would like to thank him for all he has done for our profession." And now, at the end of my first day of teaching at BYU, before I was even unpacked, here was an invitation to meet Dr. Bergin!

I walked down the hall and around the corner to his office. The note had failed to mention that Dr. Bergin was also President Bergin—president of the BYU 5th Stake. Within moments of meeting, we were both in tears as he called me to be the stake Relief Society president of that stake over which he presided. What a thrill it was for me to serve under his priesthood keys, and then, when he was released, under those of President Truman Madsen.

Brother Madsen had been my spiritual mentor, again without ever knowing it because I had never met *him* in person either. But his teachings about Joseph Smith had stirred my soul for years.

I well remember the morning I determined that I never wanted to teach one more class or conduct one more clinical supervision session without knowing that the Holy Ghost was with me. As much as I loved music, it felt too precarious to leave my spiritual and emotional preparations of the day to a disc jockey who could influence my thoughts and feelings through the music she or he might select. *That* was the day I decided to listen to Book of Mormon tapes or Truman Madsen tapes as I got ready for and traveled to work.

Now, just for a moment, let's circle back to my early days of teaching at BYU. Note to self: *Just because something is right doesn't mean it is going to be easy.*

As much as I loved my teaching at BYU and my calling as stake Relief Society president, there was *so much* to learn. So much to *do.* I felt overwhelmed. And often I felt so alone. For the first several months, my morning routine included starting my Book of Mormon tapes, turning on the shower, getting into the shower, and—crying.

I discovered that the shower was such a great place to let out my emotions. The sound of the water covered my sobbing. I could wash my face and wash my tears away at the same time. That was so efficient. And my tears went down the drain. That was so tidy.

As the days and months rolled on, the tears slowed. Not often, but from time to time, I would think about the words I had heard when entering the Taylor Building: "It's not about the job." For example, when I would be offered an unexpected opportunity to serve on a committee or meet a new person, I would think, *Oh, it's not about the job, it's about being chair of BYU's Women's Conference.* And life would go on.

Remember that pivotal day in my life—April 6, 1992—when I telephoned BYU to follow through with my prompting from that April general conference? *Fourteen years later,* I would finally participate in the reason the Lord brought me to BYU. Indeed, it was *not* about the job. It was about marrying Elder Russell M. Nelson and being sealed as husband and wife in the Salt Lake Temple on April 6, 2006, by President Gordon B. Hinckley.

My husband likens the Lord's orchestration of bringing me from Canada to Utah, for the express reason to be by his side, to the way the Lord orchestrated moving the Smith family from Sharon, Vermont, to Palmyra, New York, so that Joseph Smith could be near the Hill Cumorah. Although that may be an overstatement prompted by the grateful feelings of a husband in love with his wife, I do know the Lord was the one who brought us together as a couple. The Lord was definitely our matchmaker. And it all started when I took a question to April 1992 general conference. The heavens opened, bringing me three letters, *B-Y-U,* that changed my life.

CHAPTER 9

CELEBRATE THE ATONEMENT OF JESUS CHRIST EVERY DAY

You and I know that *the* most important event that ever occurred—in this or any other world—is the Atonement of Jesus Christ. Therefore, His Atonement should be the most important event in each of *our* lives. Easter is the traditional time for Christians around the world to commemorate the atoning sacrifice of Jesus Christ. But true Latter-day Saints, as disciples of Jesus Christ, commemorate the Atonement of our Savior far more than just once a year.

We know that the Savior's Atonement includes three principal events:

First, the Savior's Atonement includes His incomprehensible suffering in the Garden of Gethsemane, which suffering caused Him literally to bleed at every pore. Through that extreme suffering, He paid for *all* the sins, *all* the infirmities, *all* the suffering, *all* of the pain of all of us—and *of each one of us*—including the sins, infirmities, suffering, and pain of those who will *never* choose to repent, who will *never* accept the Savior's infinite offering. Think of that!

I have been to the place known as the Garden of Gethsemane. I have walked the paths and seen the gnarled trees. I've tried to imagine what it was like for our Savior there. Of course, that is impossible. But I have felt the solemn spirit of that sacred place.

Second, the Savior's Atonement includes His Crucifixion—during which time all the incomprehensible mental anguish, the immeasurable emotional grief, and the unimaginable physical pain of Gethsemane *returned* to Him—*and* He experienced the most heart-wrenching trial of all, expressed in His lament, "My God, my God, why hast thou forsaken me?" (Matthew 27:46). Again, it is impossible for our mortal minds to imagine any of that, including the horrors of the wounds from the spear in the Savior's side and the prints of the nails in His hands and feet as He hung on the cross of Calvary. I've been to the place where they say the Savior was crucified. I've read and reread teachings from Elder James E. Talmage and others about the Savior's

Crucifixion. But the enormity of that crucial event in our Heavenly Father's plan of salvation is totally incomprehensible to me.

What happens to each of us when the reality of the Savior's Atonement begins to settle—even slightly—upon our hearts and minds? What are we drawn to do differently in our lives?

What happens to us when we realize just a bit more that Jesus Christ was *the only One* who was willing and able to endure all of Gethsemane and all of Calvary? Only *He* could make it possible for us to return Home clean to our Heavenly Parents—as we choose to repent.

There is no way for our finite minds to comprehend fully the depth of Christ's infinite *love* for us—the love that motivated Him to endure Gethsemane and Golgotha. But we can thank Him by *always* remembering what He did for us. This is what we promise when we worthily partake of the sacrament, and by living in such a manner that His Atonement becomes the greatest reality of our lives.

Third, the Savior's Atonement includes His literal and glorious Resurrection from the garden tomb. The body and spirit of Jesus Christ were truly reunited, never to be separated again. As attested to by many eyewitnesses,[19] our Savior Jesus Christ has

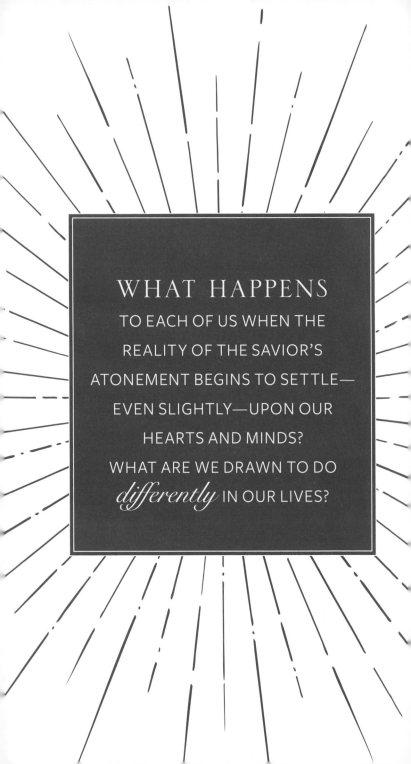

WHAT HAPPENS
TO EACH OF US WHEN THE
REALITY OF THE SAVIOR'S
ATONEMENT BEGINS TO SETTLE—
EVEN SLIGHTLY—UPON OUR
HEARTS AND MINDS?
WHAT ARE WE DRAWN TO DO
differently IN OUR LIVES?

an incorruptible body of flesh and bone. He is *not* merely a spirit.

I have visited the garden tomb. And it's true! His tomb is empty. I've seen where He was laid. He is not there.

He rose on that third day, breaking the bands of death for *billions* of His Father's children. For all of them. For each one of them. For you and for me. Could there be a greater cause for celebration than the reality of the Resurrection?

The Lord instituted the ordinance of the sacrament to provide us with an opportunity to ponder frequently on the sacrifice of His body and His blood. He entreats us, "Behold the wounds which pierced my side, and also the prints of the nails in my hands and feet" (Doctrine and Covenants 6:37).

And in anticipation of the difficulties in our lives—knowing full well the vexing situations we presently face or will yet face—the Savior tells us how to get through each and every one of our troubles and trials. He says, "Look unto me in *every* thought" (Doctrine and Covenants 6:36).

That is the solution to *whatever* problem you and I have or will ever have. Look unto the Savior in *every* thought. And, I'm pretty sure that when Jesus Christ says "every thought," He means *every thought,* including every happy thought, every despairing thought, every grateful thought, every unworthy thought, every "I-can't-do-this-one-more-moment" thought.

Could it really be true that the answer to *every one* of our problems, *every* obstacle, *every* difficulty, *everything* that is unfair, *every* false accusation, and *each and every* impossible situation in our lives is to look to the Savior, to remember Him and what He has done for us? Yes! The answer is to remember and celebrate the Atonement of Jesus Christ.

For decades I've loved the counsel recorded in Hebrews 12:1–2. It begins: "Let us lay aside every weight . . ." I remember the first day that scripture spoke to me. I was on vacation with friends but was sitting by myself on a picnic table near a beach. There were many things weighing me down that day. What is weighing *you* down?

The author continues, " . . . and the sin which doth so easily beset us . . ." What sin—of omission or commission—keeps wrecking your life? What sin— of omission or commission—is preventing you from becoming the woman or man of God, the true disciple of Jesus Christ you were born to be?

After telling us to lay aside everything that is weighing us down and every sin, the author then tells us how to do that: "Looking unto Jesus the author and finisher of our faith; who for the joy that was set before him endured the cross."

Again, this is the one and only solution to *every* trouble in our lives. This absolute cure-all is so effective that the Savior tells us that *as* we remember Him, *as* we look to Him, and *as* we remember what He has done for us, we will have no reason to doubt or to fear. Jesus Christ says: "Look unto me in every thought; doubt not, fear not" (Doctrine and Covenants 6:36).

As we truly focus on the Savior, as we truly remember Him and His infinite Atonement, as day after day we think of Him more and more, the heavens *will* open. Our fears and doubts will decrease. Some will even flee! We will be led along. We will know what to do, step by step. We will learn how to draw upon the power available to us because the Savior atoned for us. We will learn how to access His cleansing, healing, redemptive, strengthening power. And we will experience the freedom to be our true selves as we unyoke ourselves from the world and instead yoke ourselves to the Savior.

Question: How can we diligently, consistently, daily seek to feel the power of Jesus Christ every day of our lives?

• We can study truths about the Savior and His Atonement that we've never studied before. At times this might mean reading extensively in the scriptures, but at other times it might mean pondering over just a few verses for hours or days or even weeks. The heavens opened for President Joseph F. Smith on October 3, 1918, when he "sat in [his] room pondering over the scriptures; and reflecting upon the great atoning sacrifice that was made by the Son of God, for the redemption of the world" (Doctrine and Covenants 138:1–2). And the heavens can open for us as we follow that same pattern. As President Smith explained, "The eyes of my understanding were opened, and the Spirit of the Lord rested upon me" (v. 11). Similarly, the eyes of our understanding can be opened, and the Spirit of the Lord can rest upon *us,* again as we do what President Smith did: as *we* ponder over the scriptures and as *we* reflect upon the Atonement of Jesus Christ. And then, what will happen for us will be exactly what the Lord knows we are ready to experience.

• We can fast in a way that brings forth the kind of blessings of which Isaiah spoke when he wrote Messianically: "Is not this the fast that I have chosen? to loose the bands of wickedness, to undo the heavy burdens, and to let the oppressed go free, and that ye break every yoke?" (Isaiah 58:6). Could you, or someone you love, be blessed by having the bands of wickedness loosened or heavy burdens taken off? Is there someone you love, or you yourself, who feels oppressed and longs to be free, who feels constrained by the yoke that is presently upon him or her? Fasting, true fasting the way the Lord has taught, can open the heavens and bring each of those blessings to your life or to the lives of those you love.

• We can *pray* to be able to think of the Savior more. We can pray and learn to think of Him in *whatever* we are doing.

• We can make sacrifices of time to the Lord by worshipping and serving in the temple and by finding qualifying information to allow those who now live on the other side of the veil to receive temple blessings. They now know *firsthand* the necessity and eternal efficacy of making covenants with God and receiving essential ordinances. No wonder they urge us on.

Through these and other experiences, we can celebrate the Atonement of Jesus Christ *every day*. This most important event in the history of this world—or any other world—will then become the greatest reality of our lives, and the heavens will open for us more than they ever have before!

CHAPTER 10

FIND YOUR ANCESTORS

When you hear the words *family history,* do you go into a coma? Believe me, until a few years ago, I could have matched my coma with yours any day. It used to be that if I wanted to have a really good sleep, all I needed to do was to *think* about doing family history work. Just the prospect of doing it was better than ether!

But now, for me, there is not a faster way to have the heavens open than to pray to be led to those who live on the other side of the veil who have accepted the gospel of Jesus Christ and are eager to make covenants with God and receive their essential ordinances.

After years, even decades, of carting boxes of family history materials to one apartment or condo

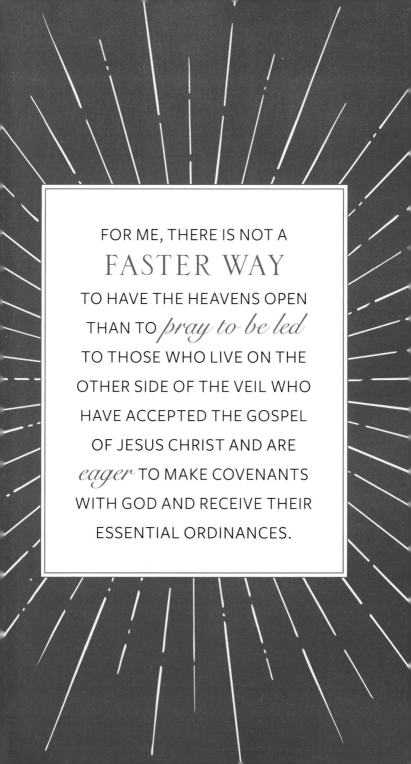

FOR ME, THERE IS NOT A *FASTER WAY* TO HAVE THE HEAVENS OPEN THAN TO *pray to be led* TO THOSE WHO LIVE ON THE OTHER SIDE OF THE VEIL WHO HAVE ACCEPTED THE GOSPEL OF JESUS CHRIST AND ARE *eager* TO MAKE COVENANTS WITH GOD AND RECEIVE THEIR ESSENTIAL ORDINANCES.

after another, in December 2012 I was finally ready to take the plunge into family history research in an entirely different way. The impetus for me was a message by Elder Richard G. Scott in his October 2012 general conference address, "The *Joy* of Redeeming the Dead."[20] When Elder Scott spoke, it felt as though he was speaking directly to me and allowing fifteen million others to listen in. At the end of his talk, when he said, "What about you? Have you prayed about your own ancestors' work?" I heard it as, "What about you, Wendy? Have you prayed about your ancestors' work?"

No, I hadn't. And I hadn't even thought about doing so. The thing I had done *the very most* about my ancestors was to feel guilty. I had done a lot of that!

But on this December morning in 2012, I was ready to do more than feel guilty. I was ready to do more than attempt to "organize" the family history records my grandmother had bequeathed to me. I was ready to have the heavens open to help me find my ancestors. As my husband and I read the Book of Mormon that morning, I noticed several mentions of the word *durst*.

Durst. The word stirred something in me. That word is used eighteen times in the book of Alma. At the time it seemed far more than eighteen times. It felt like *durst* was every other word. And every time my husband and I would read the word *durst,* I had the same unusual feeling.

A few days later, I happened to open an old notebook of my grandmother's containing genealogical information in her own handwriting. The first name I saw was that of Kathryn *Durst*!

I wasn't sure what to do with that name, but I was ready to find out. To say I was a beginner would be an understatement. The first time I opened the FamilySearch website and, with a friend on the other end of the phone coaching me, tried to learn how to use it, it was a disaster. At one point I said, "At this moment my computer screen doesn't look like anything you are describing." I thanked her, hung up, and fell to my knees and pled: "I don't know how to do any of this. If this is important, please help me."

That prayer was the first small step in opening the heavens for me with regard to family history research. Little by little, as I began to understand some of the basics of the FamilySearch website, I also began to experience what Elder Scott taught when he said that family history is "a monumental effort of cooperation on both sides of the veil, where help is given in both directions."[21] Over and over again during the first few years, I was amazed to just "happen" to meet a person who could help me learn more about how to research names more productively. And I never take it for granted when, seemingly out of the blue, I find a piece of information I need. There is no doubt in my mind that angels from both sides of the veil are assigned to help us with this work and that we are rarely, if ever, alone in our efforts to find family names and prepare them for sacred temple ordinances.

So, what do we need so we can do our part in family history work? What is it that we don't understand? The first step is to ask. Ask. Ask. Ask. Pray. Pray. Pray. And then follow each and every prompting.

I have learned that my family history research goes better when I kneel and begin with prayer. Many involved in family history research have come to believe, as I do, that our ancestors know where their own records are and that they will help us find those records.

Let me share just two such experiences, as I recorded them.

"March 20, 2016: Day of Provo City Center Temple dedication.

"Record of William Townley on top of pile of papers on my desk by computer. I had not put it there.

"Opened to 'Person' on FamilySearch and it opened right to him! I had not been working there.

"I looked to see why William Townley was so eager for me to find him.

"Answer: several of his children—three, actually—had been overlooked. They needed their ordinances completed."

A few days later, still in March 2016, I recorded the following regarding a different man whose first name was also William:

"William Henry Thompson: There were four choices for a wife that fit with his name and the time he lived and even the location where he lived.

"I was confused and said out loud: 'You're going to have to help me.' Suddenly, the computer screen showed his marriage record. It was not there before. I had scrolled through all the offerings that Ancestry.com had given—several pages—and I had never been able to find his marriage record. And now—here it was."

Those who have never felt the opening of heaven that doing family history research can bring may doubt—even scoff at—these experiences. I can only attest that these kinds of discoveries happen again and again. Because of one experience after another, I have come to believe that making a sacrifice of time

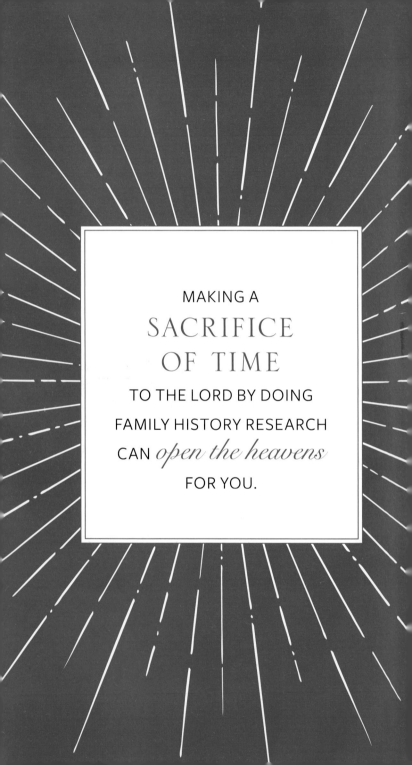

MAKING A

SACRIFICE
OF TIME

TO THE LORD BY DOING

FAMILY HISTORY RESEARCH

CAN *open the heavens*

FOR YOU.

to the Lord by doing family history research can open the heavens for you.

Here is another family history research note I made:

"*April 1, 2019*

"*In six years of doing family history research, I found* one *person born in Italy—a man who married a young woman from the United States of America.*

"*Now, since the Rome Italy Temple dedication [March 2019], I can't work fast enough or long enough to keep up with the records I am finding for those born in Italy! I have found many—at least one hundred in just a few days—and I don't know how I even got on that limb of our family tree. I can feel that they are excited. They had been sitting there—just waiting, more like longing, for someone to find their information and do their ordinance work.*"

There is *always* an urgency associated with this work.[22] That is what I feel when I am spiritually in tune with heaven. It is exactly as Elder Scott said, "This is a spiritual work."

However, since the dedication of the temple in Rome, something new has been added to that feeling of urgency. I would almost call it a *clamoring*. This is a new experience for me. (Perhaps it is many expressive, energetic Italians rejoicing on the other side of the veil.) As one ordinance worker said to me in the temple at the completion of an ordinance: "Oh, there is going to be dancing in heaven tonight!"

So, if you are wondering if your prayers are heard, if you are longing for the heavens to open for you, may I suggest that you commence your family history research efforts with a prayer to be led to those who are ready to make covenants and receive their ordinances? And then, in an exercise of faith, expect for spiritual adventures to follow. It is my experience that family history research will make any extreme sport or high adventure activity pale in comparison.

Now, there are those who may call my desire to help gather Israel on the other side of the veil an addiction. I disagree. An addiction is something negative that ruins a person's life. Family history research, which involves working with the heavens, lifts me, strengthens me, puts other things in my life into perspective for me, increases my ability to be guided by the Spirit, and brings me personal revelation and such *joy*! And all of those things help me to be a better wife and help our home to be a place of refuge, rejuvenation, and revelation.

Here's one more notation from my family history

research journal. It demonstrates just how eager our ancestors are for their work to be completed:

"I just found this man. It's his birthday today. September 29.

"But what is more exciting and points out just how invested he was in my finding him—is that it was exactly 110 years ago today that he was born!! So literally today is the first day *that he qualifies for proxy baptism."*

Oh, yes indeed, our ancestors want their work done!

An email I sent recently to my sisters demonstrates how deeply I feel about the power of family history research to open the heavens and bless our lives:

"I wish all the doubters would take the time they spend on the internet doing their 'research' about the Church (really, against *the Church) and spend that same amount of time on the FamilySearch website. If they would combine their research with prayer, they would experience just how* real *those on the other side are, and how* eager—even desperate—*those ancestors are for their proxy ordinances to be done. At that point, the faith of those who once were doubting would become unshaken. That's what I believe."*

Prayer and family history research open the

heavens for me. In fact, I have learned to keep a pad of paper beside me as I'm working on family history to record ideas that flow into my mind and heart to help me in *other* areas of my life. I testify that the same blessing can come to you as you work to find your ancestors. The heavens will open!

CHAPTER 11

TESTIMONY OF AN EYEWITNESS

Tuesday, January 2, 2018, started out as a tender but wonderful day for my husband and me. In the morning, I spoke at the funeral of one of our dear friends. She was 100 years old and had remained vibrant and steadfast in the gospel of Jesus Christ to the end! As his meetings for the new year had not yet commenced, my husband accompanied me to the funeral. Afterward, we attended the temple.

We rounded out our day with a little shopping, worked at home on several time-sensitive projects for the new year, and then called it a day and went to bed early.

At 11:01 p.m., we were awakened by a phone call telling us of the passing of President Thomas S. Monson. We were stunned!

My husband and I talked for quite a while, made a few phone calls, and then turned out the lights.

As I stared out into the dark of the night and into our future, the hymn that came to my mind was, "Where Can I Turn for Peace?" And I have to confess that—just for a moment—my mind raced straight to the line, "Where can I run?" (In that moment I had *such* empathy for Jonah!)

On March 31, 2018, I wondered how I would feel as I gathered with 21,000 Saints in the Conference Center in Salt Lake City for the solemn assembly in which my husband would be sustained as President of the Church. I was prepared to feel a little anxious, but instead, I felt something I never expected: an overwhelming feeling of peace. I felt like I was actually *immersed* in peace.

The peace I experienced the morning of the solemn assembly was not of *this* world. It was provided by the Prince of Peace, Jesus the Christ. I personally experienced the Savior's promise: "Peace I leave with you, my peace I give unto you" (John 14:27).

Right from the beginning, *only* the Lord could help my husband and me deal with *many* new things. Some things changed immediately: our ability to come and go as we had all of our lives ceased, our calendaring became more complicated, our visibility increased, and our privacy decreased dramatically.

Other changes, however, were more meaningful and important. There is an old saying that "the wife is the last to know." In the case of President Nelson's becoming the Lord's prophet to the world, I will be eternally grateful that the Lord intervened so that I was *not* the last to know.

Just two days after President Monson departed from this mortal life, the Lord gave me a unique, most distinctive experience with my husband to let *me* know that the mantle of prophet was upon him. It was so vivid, so clear, so real! *Every* detail of that experience was seared into my mind and heart.

Then, two days later, the Lord gave me *exactly* the same experience again. That experience—repeated twice—is too sacred for me to share, but it is one that I can neither forget nor deny.

Because of that sacred experience, repeated twice,[23] I can take any witness stand in any nation on earth to testify that I know President Russell Marion Nelson has been called by God to be the living prophet of the Lord on the earth today.

Other things changed as well. During our nearly twelve years of marriage—to that point—I had become accustomed to my husband's being awakened

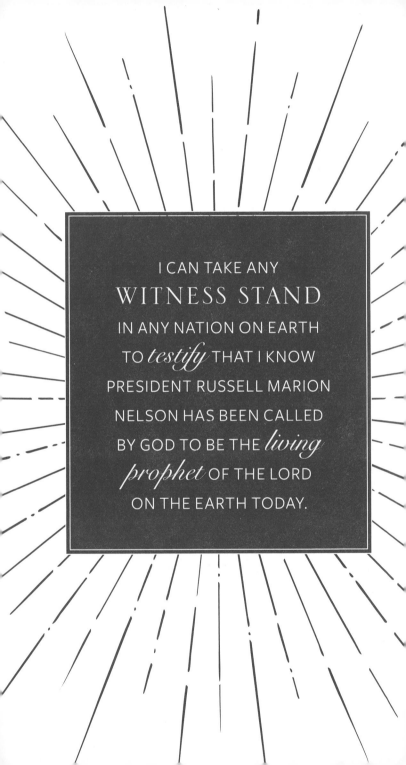

I CAN TAKE ANY
WITNESS STAND
IN ANY NATION ON EARTH
TO *testify* THAT I KNOW
PRESIDENT RUSSELL MARION
NELSON HAS BEEN CALLED
BY GOD TO BE THE *living*
prophet OF THE LORD
ON THE EARTH TODAY.

during the night with ideas for general conference talks and refinements to them. But since he became President of the Church, the number of nighttime interruptions from heaven has increased exponentially!

The impressions he receives are private, for him and the leaders of the Church to discuss. We never discuss them. But I am usually aware when he slips out of the room to record the information he's receiving. The sheer frequency of these nighttime experiences has allowed me to witness how willing the Lord is to talk to His prophet. I do indeed believe *all* that God will *yet* reveal (see Articles of Faith 1:9).

One early Saturday morning not long after President Monson's passing was unforgettable. I was awakened earlier than I wanted to be awake, and I had a strong prompting to leave the room. *Now!* I did so and worked on several projects in other rooms in our home.

Two hours later, my husband emerged from our bedroom and said, "Wendy, you won't believe what has been happening for the past two hours since you left," indicating that the Lord had been tutoring him.

So, I am a witness by being present, and I am a witness by being absent, that the Lord indeed instructs His prophet.

Let me share with you another observation: Since

my husband was called as President of the Church, it has been quite an experience to send him off to work because, on *many* days, at the end of a rigorous day for him of meetings and decisions at Church headquarters, the man I greet at the end of the day is just a little different from the man I kissed good-bye in the morning.

What are some of those changes? Well, right off the top, he is even more loving and just a little more filled with joy!

His vigor and enthusiasm for the Lord's work increase day after day.

Another change is that I've seen him look even younger right on the spot. For example, at a gathering in Canada, as my husband became increasingly connected with the congregation while delivering the message of his heart, I watched what seemed like thirty years fall away right in that moment at the pulpit!

And I can tell you that, as he is now well into his tenth decade of life, my husband is becoming even *more* of his true self every day! Why wouldn't he be? He is now doing exactly what he was foreordained to do.

I appreciate something Elder Bruce R. McConkie (a departed member of the Quorum of the Twelve) said about President Spencer W. Kimball, the Lord's twelfth prophet of this dispensation. I believe Elder McConkie's words can apply to all of the Lord's prophets, including President Nelson.

"[Premortally, he] knew and worshiped the Lord Jehovah. . . . He was a friend of Adam and Enoch. He took counsel from Noah and Abraham. He sat in meetings with Isaiah and Nephi. He served in the heavenly kingdom with Joseph Smith and Brigham Young."[24]

It is my testimony that President Russell M. Nelson was foreordained to be the Lord's prophet on the earth today to help gather Israel, on both sides of the veil, and to help prepare the Church—and the world—for the Second Coming of our Savior Jesus Christ.

Everything in The Church of Jesus Christ of Latter-day Saints belongs to Jesus Christ. The doctrine is His, the covenants are His, ordinances are His, priesthood power is His power. The Apostles are His. And the prophet is *His* prophet, chosen and instructed by Him. The heavens truly are open, and revelation flows freely—as we seek it. Of that I testify.

CHAPTER 12

PRAY

I've always been struck with how generous the Lord is with His knowledge—*if* we seek it. There's not a better time in any of our lives to "grow into the principle of revelation"[25] than when we are *desperate* to know the answer to a question that has great implications and ramifications for our lives. Questions such as: "Should I marry this person?" "Should I move?" "Should I pursue my education?" "Should I take this job?" Why would we ever settle for the best answers that the world can give us when the Lord stands ready to open the heavens to teach us, mentor us, and speak to us through the whisperings of the Spirit? Personal revelation is something we each want and need.

Recently my husband said to me, "Wendy, the Lord is just as eager to give revelation to you as He is to give it to me." I've understood that principle for most of my life, but it was wonderful to have President Nelson spontaneously confirm that great truth, which truth applies to each one of us. The Lord is just as eager to give revelation to *you* for your life as He is to give revelation to His prophet for His Church!

When we are willing to "do the spiritual work required to enjoy the gift of the Holy Ghost and hear the voice of the Spirit more frequently and more clearly," as President Nelson counseled, our "spiritual capacity to receive revelation"[26] will increase, and we will be led to know what the Lord would have us do.

In this day and age particularly, why would any of us go to the internet for the answer to *anything* that will affect our lives here and hereafter? Admittedly, we can find fascinating as well as useful information online about everything from the words of a poem or song we love to how to roast vegetables to the best place nearby to buy a falafel. But we can also encounter blatant, intentional lies disguised as truth, as well as tons of incorrect information and misinformation.

And, all the while, the heavens are open 24-7! Our Heavenly Father awaits our prayers.

I had a particularly desperate need of my own some years ago that required some serious spiritual work on my part to entreat the heavens to open for me.

There is no possible way that this can be right!

That was my thought on an early Monday morning as I drove out of the city where I lived at the time. I needed some peace and quiet, and a little time alone, to seek an answer to a major question that had arisen in my life.

For several weeks, Elder Russell M. Nelson, a member of the Quorum of the Twelve Apostles, had been making overtures to get to know me better. His wife, Dantzel, had been deceased for a period of time, and as of late—and at his instigation—we had exchanged books that we had each authored, written a couple of notes to each other, and spoken on the phone a few times.

I had a history of dating wonderful men, getting close to marriage, and then breaking up, or, in several cases, breaking the engagement. I did *not* want to do that again—and certainly not when it involved an Apostle! And from a more practical standpoint, I wondered, *How do you "date" an Apostle?* I had no idea. The prospect seemed inconceivable to me—and entirely out of the question.

I had to figure out if I should allow this relationship to move forward or not. And I felt that I needed to figure it out *before* investing myself in the relationship. How was I going to do that? I didn't want to pick up one end of this stick unless I was supposed to pick up the other. I knew that the Lord knew the answer. All I had to do was to find out what *He* knew about this relationship, to find out what His will was for me.

Several months before Elder Nelson contacted me, I had been praying, "Please help me to fill the measure of my creation." Initially, I had been a bit hesitant to ask. Was I really ready for the answer? Was I serious about doing *whatever* the Lord wanted, even needed, me to do? I took a deep breath and commenced.

Over time, as I daily continued that prayer, I was led to pray for my unknown husband in a very real way. I was not just praying, "Please help me find my husband," but praying *for* my husband: "Please help my husband today." I had never prayed like that before in my life.

I didn't know who my husband was. I didn't have a clue. But I was pretty sure he would be widowed. I also had the feeling that he would have loving, attentive children who would be missing their departed mother and pouring all their love for their parents into caring for, nurturing, and shoring up their father. So my prayers included pleas such as: "Please help my husband have a great day today. Comfort him and strengthen him. Help his children to draw close to him and take care of him as he grieves for his wife and their mother."

My praying and seeking prompted me to write a letter to my unknown husband—again, something I had never done before. In the letter, I told him that even though I didn't know who he was, I knew a lot about him. For example, I knew that he loved the Lord, loved the temple, loved the scriptures, loved his departed wife, loved his children. I went on and on telling my unknown husband everything I knew about his marvelous qualities.

Suffice it to say, the Lord had been laying the groundwork for the big question I was facing that day as I headed out of the city to seek some peace and quiet.

The next day, I fasted, immersed myself in the scriptures, and poured out my heart in prayer. I did this from early in the morning until about 4:00 p.m. Then the heavens opened, bringing me a message I *never* expected. In three different ways, I received a very distinct message. To this moment I can feel the power and clarity with which the Lord let me know

His will for my potential relationship with Elder Russell M. Nelson.

I did *not* expect this answer and certainly had no idea of the dramatic changes into which I would be catapulted, including leaving my profession of more than three decades, moving, marrying a man twenty-six years my senior with a very large family, and joining my life with that of a man whose life was completely consecrated to the Lord.

But, as Joseph Smith said of the fact that he had seen a vision and could not deny it (see Joseph Smith—History 1:25), neither could I deny the clear message the Lord gave *me* in response to my earnest fasting, searching the scriptures, and supplications in prayer. The heavens had opened, and my life would never be the same.

While my answer came after months and months of preparation, and then several weeks of wondering, and then hours and hours of focused beseeching, my friend Lynda Wilson learned how immediately the Lord's answers can come. In fact, she learned that answers can come *in the very moment!*

Lynda's husband, Elder Larry Y. Wilson, is an emeritus General Authority Seventy who at the time was serving in the Asia Area Presidency. One day, Lynda was to speak with him at a devotional for temple workers in the Taipei Taiwan Temple. Then something unexpected happened. This is Lynda's experience, in her own words:

"As the first meeting started I felt quite relaxed and looked forward to hearing my husband's talk. Imagine my horror when he started by saying, 'I would like to share with you today a story in the Old Testament that my wife is fond of using when talking about temples.' He then proceeded to give my *entire* talk. I have never felt quite so helpless.

"There was no time between that meeting and the sisters' meeting that followed it. There was not even a break so that I could find a private place to pray a desperate prayer. There was only a short walk across a hallway and into a small room filled with white brocade chairs and the expectant faces of about fifteen beautiful Chinese sisters. I only had time during that walk across the hall to glance at the ceiling and remind heaven, 'I got nothin'.'

"But I did have a translator, a lovely young woman who would translate for me into Mandarin, sentence by sentence. And I also had enough presence of mind to thank the sisters for the opportunity to speak to them and to tell them how beautiful I thought their temple was. I said that much and stopped, waiting as the translator spoke my words again in their language.

"While my translator was speaking, a small thought just sort of fluttered down into my mind. Like a string of small white feathers came these six words: 'The world is a noisy place.' As I already told you, I had nothing, so I decided to speak those six words, and I said aloud, 'The world is a noisy place.'

"Then I had to stop and give the translator time to repeat those words in the Chinese language. And while she was speaking, it happened again. One sentence floated down into my consciousness: 'But My voice is a still, small voice.'

"I repeated that blessed sentence word for word, amazed but happily willing to be part of the little miracle unfolding before me. I gave the entire talk like that. The Lord was teaching the sisters about the need for holy, quiet places in their lives where they could commune with Him and receive comfort and instruction from the Holy Spirit, in the temple or in their 'prayer closets.'

"I spoke for about ten minutes, and other than the general outline I just gave you, I could not now tell you any other specific thing that I said. I do remember, however, that it was well received and there were tears in some eyes. Of course there were, because the Spirit had been there in abundance, testifying of truth and propping up a very grateful servant who, ten minutes before, 'had nothing.'"

Sometimes our prayers are answered like Lynda's, in the very moment. Often we don't have any idea what the answer to our prayer might be. And at other times, we need to "begin with the end in mind," as President Nelson often declares. It seems that is how God answers many of our prayers. Have you noticed that He often answers according to what you *want to have happen*—rather than answering a specific request?

For example, I once asked a friend newly diagnosed with cancer, "What have you been praying for lately?"

Her answer: "I've been praying that my husband and my sons will want to spend more time at home, get along better with each other, and be more helpful around our home."

My next question: "What has happened since you have been diagnosed with cancer?"

You know her answer. Her husband and sons wanted to be home more, were getting along better with each other, and were so helpful that my friend wondered what someone had done with the man she married and with her sons!

All the things she had been praying for happened—*following* her diagnosis with cancer.

Perhaps there is a message for us in this example that will help us with our prayers. When we are praying to know what to do, or praying to help someone know what to do (for example: whether they should move to a different city or not), perhaps the heavens respond and open most readily when we pray along the lines of "Please help them to draw closer to Thee and Thy Son" (the desired end result), rather than "Please help them sell their home" (a specific request). This is not to say that we shouldn't pray for specific requests. Of course we should. But from time to time, see what happens as you pray for yourself or others to draw closer to Heavenly Father and Jesus Christ. Notice what happens as you pray with *that* end in mind.

What does *the Lord* want to have happen in your life? As we live to see things increasingly as the Lord sees them, we will be led along, even in our prayers to Him. He knows what will be best. Even knowing this, we sometimes have a hard time emulating the Savior's prayer, "Thy will be done."

My mother coped with the effects of mini-strokes for several years. When blindness was layered on top of her already diminished physical capacities,

SEE WHAT HAPPENS
AS YOU PRAY FOR YOURSELF
OR OTHERS TO *draw closer*
TO HEAVENLY FATHER AND
JESUS CHRIST. NOTICE WHAT
HAPPENS AS YOU PRAY
WITH *that* END IN MIND.

we brought in all the available health-care services and the best professionals we could find. For several years I prayed: "Please help Mom not fall today," "Please help us find the right medical care to help her," "Please help us know what else we can do to bring joy to her life," and so on.

Then one Sunday I found myself praying differently about my mother than I ever had before. I prayed that day, *"Thy will be done."* By the next Sunday my mother was alive and well! She could do *all* the things that brought her such joy. She could see and walk and sing, and so much more—because now she was living on the other side of the veil.

When my sisters and I visited together after Mom's funeral, we discovered that even though we lived in three different cities and had never talked with each other about this, each one of us had been prompted to fast and pray "Thy will be done" on that *very same* Sunday in March.

That's when I started to think about the possible reciprocity between our prayers and heaven's desires for us. Are we really supplicating the Lord for what *we* think we need and want, or, if we are in tune, is heaven *prompting us* to ask for things *the Lord* wants for us? When we pray "Thy will be done," we let the Lord know we are ready to receive *whatever* He is ready to give to us. Or perhaps *whatever* He knows we are finally ready to receive.

That reminds me of a prayer offered by a dear friend. One day my future husband asked me to find a home for us. Only a few people knew we were engaged, so he couldn't go looking for a home. We weren't ready for the rumors.

Our friend went house hunting with me, and I found a home I liked immediately. I could see all kinds of possibilities for my husband-to-be and me. I asked our friend if she would quickly offer a prayer that Elder Nelson and I could own this home.

She did. But she changed the words! She prayed, "Please help Elder Nelson and Wendy to acquire this home—or something better."

As I drove to my home, I kept remembering the words: *or something better*. I phoned our friend and said, "Do you always pray that way? I never knew you could add that little tagline—'or something better.'" She laughed, never really answering my question.

Later that evening, those unusual words were still lingering in my mind: *or something better*. I called our friend: "Do you know who else prayed for *something better?* The Prophet Joseph Smith!"

We recalled together the story of Joseph Smith

and Emma sitting down to a meager meal of corn-bread. The Prophet prayed, "Lord, we thank Thee for this johnny cake, and ask Thee to bring us *something better*." Moments later, there was a knock on the door. It was a man bringing some flour and a ham to the Smiths.[27]

Is there *something better* that the Lord would bring to us if we would let Him know that we are seeking His will for us, and His will alone? What would help us to grow spiritually to the point that we want *only* whatever the Lord would deem to be *something better* for us? *Something* that is so much *better* than we even know to ask?

I should add, as a postscript, that the next time I went house hunting, after the *something better* prayer by our friend, the Lord led me to a home that was far more suited to the needs of my husband and me. It was indeed *something better.*

Over the years I have apologized to the Lord for some of my prayers. Many times I have prayed for something—and then have not done my part. I'm sorry about that. The Lord is not a magician. And that's how I've treated Him in those instances. However, the Lord does bring miracles to our lives— *when* we do our part. I've experienced that over and over again.

I've apologized for my prayers that were born of my mortal shortsightedness—often influenced by my blatant selfishness. I have been known to ask for things that, if given, could have been disastrous! Heavenly Father has been *so* kind to me, and forgiving, either by saying no or by not responding and just overlooking how naive I was about what I thought would bless my life.

I'm so grateful for the scripture that tells us how to receive that for which we ask. The Lord says, "And whatsoever ye shall ask the Father in my name, *which is right,* believing that ye shall receive, behold it shall be given unto you" (3 Nephi 18:20; emphasis added).

I love those words, *which is right.* Because I have asked for things which were *not.*

How different are our prayers when we pray to know that which the Lord would have us pray? How different are our lives when we pray, "Thy will be done"? We are trying to live so we can increasingly ask what the Lord would have us ask. The more the heavens are open to us because of the choices we are making in our lives, the more we will not "ask amiss" (James 4:3).

Revelation is real. Each one of us can experience that for ourselves. At the conclusion of one of the most revelatory meetings in his life, the Prophet

Joseph Smith said, "There was nothing made known to these men but what will be made known to all the Saints of the last days, so soon as they are prepared to receive."[28]

How can we prepare ourselves to receive *all* that our Heavenly Father and Jesus Christ are ready to teach us? I pray that as you have read this book, the Spirit has borne witness of something you can do— perhaps starting today—that will begin to open the heavens for you, or to open them more than they have ever been open for you before.

Like so many, I too have been affected by these words from President Nelson: "I urge you to stretch beyond your current spiritual ability to receive personal revelation, for the Lord has promised that 'if thou shalt [seek], thou shalt receive revelation upon revelation, knowledge upon knowledge, that thou mayest know the mysteries and peaceable things— that which bringeth joy, that which bringeth life eternal' [Doctrine and Covenants 42:61]."[29]

All I have witnessed, all I have experienced tells me that our Father wants to communicate with each one of His children and will do so commensurate with our desire and earnest seeking. My heart is stirred by the counsel of the Lord's prophet:

"Nothing opens the heavens quite like the

combination of increased purity, exact obedience, earnest seeking, daily feasting on the words of Christ in the Book of Mormon, and regular time committed to temple and family history work."[30]

And thus we can "learn from vaulted skies."[31]

NOTES

1. Neal A. Maxwell, "Irony: The Crust on the Bread of Adversity," *Ensign,* May 1989.

2. Michael McLean, "What I Need," © 1999 Shining Star Music (ASCAP). Used by permission.

3. Joseph Smith, *Teachings of Presidents of the Church: Joseph Smith* (2007), 267.

4. For ideas on how to do this, see Wendy Watson Nelson, *Change Your Questions, Change Your Life* (2011), 133–52.

5. Russell M. Nelson, "Sisters' Participation in the Gathering of Israel," *Ensign*, November 2018.

6. Russell M. Nelson, "'Come, Follow Me,'" *Ensign,* May 2019.

7. Henry B. Eyring, in Robert I. Eaton and Henry J. Eyring, *I Will Lead You Along: The Life of Henry B. Eyring* (2013), 40.

8. *Discourses of Brigham Young,* sel. and arr. by John A. Widtsoe (1973), 32; emphasis added.

9. Kevin McSpadden, "You Now Have a Shorter Attention Span Than a Goldfish," *Time,* May 14, 2015.

10. Alexander L. Baugh, "Parting the Veil: The Visions of Joseph Smith," *BYU Studies,* vol. 38, no. 1 (1999), 47; emphasis added.

11. Richard G. Scott, "To Acquire Spiritual Guidance," *Ensign*, November 2009.

12. Bruce R. McConkie, *A New Witness for the Articles of Faith* (1985), 259.

13. Truman G. Madsen, "The Commanding Image of Christ," BYU speech given November 16, 1965; emphasis added.

14. See Dallin H. Oaks, "Good, Better, Best," *Ensign,* November 2007.

15. Ezra Taft Benson, "Jesus Christ—Gifts and Expectations," *Ensign,* December 1988.

16. Jeffrey R. Holland, "'The Peaceable Things of the Kingdom,'" *Ensign,* November 1996.

17. Jeffrey R. Holland, "The Ministry of Reconciliation," *Ensign*, November 2018.

18. See "More Holiness Give Me," *Hymns of The Church of Jesus Christ of Latter-day Saints* (1985), no. 131.

19. See, for example, Luke 24:31, 34; John 20:27–29; 21:13–14; 1 Corinthians 15:5–8; 3 Nephi 11:13–17; Doctrine and Covenants 76:23; 110:2–4.

20. Richard G. Scott, "The Joy of Redeeming the Dead," *Ensign,* November 2012.

21. Scott, "Joy of Redeeming the Dead."

22. See Wendy Watson Nelson, *Covenant Keepers: Unlocking the Miracles God Wants for You* (2016), 52–56.

23. Actually it was repeated a third time several months later as my husband and I were reviewing an important document together.

24. "God Foreordains His Prophets and His People," *Ensign,* May 1974.

25. Joseph Smith, *Teachings: Joseph Smith,* 132.

26. Russell M. Nelson, "Revelation for the Church, Revelation for Our Lives," *Ensign,* May 2018.

27. Hyrum L. Andrus, *Joseph Smith, the Man and the Seer* (1970), 58–59; emphasis added.

28. Joseph Smith, *Teachings: Joseph Smith,* 414.

29. Nelson, "Revelation for the Church, Revelation for Our Lives."

30. Nelson, "Revelation for the Church, Revelation for Our Lives."

31. "With Humble Heart," *Hymns,* no. 171.

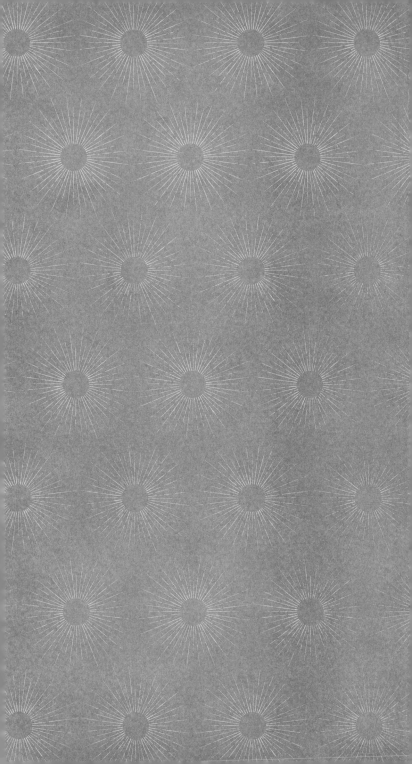